Pilgrim's Endurance
Grace Through Trials: A Bible Study
Charles E. Cravey

In His Steps Publishing

Copyright © 2025 by Charles Edward Cravey

All rights reserved.

No portion of this book may be reproduced in any form without written permission from the publisher or author, except as permitted by U.S. copyright law.

ISBN: 978-1-58535-086-5 (PAPER)

ISBN: 978-1-58535-087-2

Library of Congress Catalog Number: 2025914095

Scripture Citations:

Unless otherwise noted, all Scripture quotations are taken from the New King James Version®. Copyright © 1982 by Thomas Nelson. Used by permission. All rights reserved."

Scripture quotations marked **KJV** are from the **King James Version**. Public domain.

Printed in the United States

Published by In His Steps Publishing, Statesboro, Georgia.

Contents

Dedication	V
Introduction	VII
1. Footsteps in the Fog	1
2. Shoulders Beneath the Morning	13
3. The Fellowship of the Furnace	26
4. Grace at the Gate	36
5. Ashes Beneath the Altar	46
6. The Stream Beside the Struggle	57
7. The Wound That Worshiped	67
8. The Ledge Where Trust Was Born	78
9. The Silence Between the Psalms	88
10. The Cup That Didn't Pass	99
11. The Table in the Wilderness	109
12. Thorns in the Path	119
13. The Watchman's Light	128
14. Pilgrim's Benediction	138
Afterword	147

Dedication

To the weary who still walk,

To the praying who still wait,

To the burdened who still believe—

This book was written with you in mind.

May every chapter be a whispered thank you.

And to the One who walks beside us in silence and storm—

Introduction

"The Long Night's Journey"

Charles E. Cravey

O weary one, whose hands hang low,

Whose tread is dull, whose heart is slow,

Come trace the path where saints have gone—

Though weak, they rose and still pressed on.

For not with might did they prevail,

Nor did they fly on wings of gale.

Their strength was found beneath the weight,

Where faith walked blind and dared to wait.

The road is not for swift nor strong,

But those who cling when nights are long,

Who walk through fog with faltering breath,

Yet will not make a truce with death.

A thousand trials line this track,

And every step may press you back.

But Mercy keeps a pilgrim's pace—

And waits for you in every place.

So, lift your lamp and lift your eyes,

Though mist may mute the starlit skies,

For One walks near with nail-marked hand,

And He who called you helps you stand.

Introduction: The Worn Road

There comes a time in every believer's life when the bright certainty of early faith dims into shadow. The hymns once sung with fire feel distant. Prayers go unanswered. Days stack up with responsibilities, griefs, and delays. And though we may still believe, our feet drag. We wonder if God still walks beside us—or if He has wandered far ahead.

This is not backsliding. This is not rebellion. This is weariness.

Pilgrim's Endurance was born for such moments—for those who keep walking but feel like they're walking in fog. It is a companion to the soul who has not forsaken the journey but simply wonders how much longer the road will stretch.

The Scriptures do not flatter the spiritual path. They speak of **wilderness** (Deuteronomy 8), **pressing on through weakness** (2 Corinthians 12:9–10), and **hope deferred** (Proverbs 13:12). But through it all, they whisper the steady truth: endurance matters to God.

"Let us run with endurance the race that is set before us, fixing our eyes on Jesus…"

—**Hebrews 12:1–2**

"You have need of endurance, so that when you have done the will of God, you may receive what is promised."

—**Hebrews 10:36**

Endurance is not the denial of pain. It is the holy act of **remaining**—with faith, with tears, with limp and lamp in hand. It is not flashy. It often goes unseen. But in heaven's economy, *those who endure are crowned.*

This study is not a how-to manual. It is a quiet walk beside you, offering stories, Scripture, poetic reflections, and honest prayers for the long night. Some chapters may feel like a mirror. Others like a hand on your back.

May you discover, as so many saints before us have, that though you may feel alone, you are not unseen. Mercy walks beside you.

And though your faith feels small, it is enough to keep moving forward.

Beautiful—here's a narrative moment to follow the introduction and bring the theme of weariness and perseverance to life. It's written in your voice and tone, Charles, and invites the reader into a shared, human space:

A Pilgrim's Glimpse: When Endurance Felt Empty

I remember a Tuesday afternoon—not grand, not tragic, just gray.

I was sitting alone in a church office after everyone had gone home. The walls were too quiet. The prayer list on my desk was heavy with names I could no longer read without tears. I had preached faith for decades. Walked through hospital corridors. Buried saints and consoled mourners. And yet, in that moment, I was empty. Not unbelieving—but bone-tired of believing.

I prayed, but heaven felt brass. I opened my Bible, but the pages fluttered shut, untouched by wind. It was as if I had come to the end of everything I knew to do—and nothing stirred.

And then, a knock. Light, almost apologetic.

A young man from the church stood there, coat in hand. "I don't mean to bother you," he said, "but I felt like I was supposed to come pray for you. Is that okay?"

That moment didn't solve everything. The fog didn't lift at once. But a truth settled in deeper than emotion: I was not unseen.

Sometimes God doesn't shout from heaven—He sends footsteps to your door.

1
Footsteps in the Fog

"Footsteps in the Fog"

Charles E. Cravey

When the mists rise on all sides,
And both sun and signs obscured,
The spirit must tread where none can guide,
Except for the One whose voice is pure.

I once knew the path in clearer days,
Where streams sang sweetly and flowers bloomed.
But now the trees don ashen grays,
And every stone reveals my gloom.

The winds whisper ancient serpent tunes,
My weary feet flee their refrain—
Yet still I move forward, though fears loom,
Drawn by a light I cannot explain.

O feet, though your pace may stumble,
Keep walking, even if faith is a flicker.
The fog may be thick, but so is grace,
And Heaven acknowledges the faintest figure.

For not in haste nor strength alone,
Does the Pilgrim's crown descend from above—
But to the soul that perseveres on,
When all around it seems devoid of love.

Let me walk you into that moment...

When the Light Feels Lost and the Road Feels Long

You will walk through seasons where clarity is in short supply. Not because you've sinned. Not because God has forsaken you. But because growth often happens in the gray.

Fog, in Scripture, is rarely mentioned, but the experience is deeply biblical. Abraham left his homeland with nothing but a promise. Elijah sat under a broom tree, begging to die. David cried, "How long, O Lord?"

And Jesus Himself prayed, "My God, My God, why have You forsaken Me?"

There is a spiritual ache that comes not from rebellion, but from remaining—when the fire dims, but you still show up. And it's precisely in these places that endurance is formed. *Not in the ease of light, but in the loyalty of obscurity.*

"Even though I walk through the valley of the shadow of death, I will fear no evil, for You are with me."

—Psalm 23:4

Fog teaches trust. It strips away our obsession with direction and forces us to walk by nearness—reaching not for the path, but for the hand.

Some days, that trust will feel like a whisper. Other days, it may feel like nothing at all. But endurance doesn't always sound like a battle cry. Sometimes it's just your foot touching the path again.

Keep walking. Even when the mist clings tightly and the horizon is obscured, know that each step taken is a testament to courage. In these moments, the heart learns to listen more keenly, to seek the subtle signs of hope that linger in the air like the scent of rain on dry earth.

Remember, it is in these uncertain journeys that the soul is tempered and shaped, much like a river carving its way through stone, slowly but persistently. With every stride, you are rewriting the narrative of your resilience, painting it with the hues of quiet confidence and steadfast faith.

As the fog begins to lift, and clarity returns, you will find that you have been carried, not just by your strength, but by the unseen forces of faith and grace. So, cherish the journey, for it is not only the destination that defines you, but the steps taken in trust and hope along the way.

Each step is a brushstroke on the canvas of your life's unfolding masterpiece. Embrace the uncertainty, for it is the artist's hand guiding you through the unknown, crafting something beautiful and unique. These moments of fog are the spaces where dreams are whispered, and visions are forged in the quiet resolve of your heart.

In time, as the mist disperses and the path becomes clear once more, you'll look back on these days not with dread, but with gratitude. Gratitude for the strength you discovered, the patience you nurtured, and the faith that grew roots deep within your soul. For it is in the journey through the fog that we learn to see not just with our eyes, but with our hearts.

So, keep moving forward with the quiet assurance that you are never alone. The journey is yours, and it is blessed with every step, every stumble, and every rise. Let the fog be your teacher and the path your guide, knowing that each moment is a sacred part of your story, a tale of unwavering hope and enduring love.

A Pilgrim's Glimpse: When I Couldn't Find the Road

I recall a season when the fog was more than a metaphor.

It was the middle of winter, just before dawn, and I had taken an early morning drive through backroads carved into farmland and forest. The plan was simple: pray before sunrise at the edge of a ridge I loved. I needed direction, confirmation—some sign the work I was pouring into ministry, into writing, wasn't just a labor in vain.

But the fog was thick. Streetlights looked like flickering ghosts. The road narrowed into shadow. Every landmark I knew by heart was erased by vapor. It was disorienting and, frankly, a little frightening.

I slowed the car, turned off the music, and gripped the wheel like a lifeline. I prayed, "Lord, I can't see."

And I felt Him say—not in an audible voice, but in that soul-deep sense—*"But I still can."*

I never reached the ridge that morning. I pulled into a gravel turnout and just waited. Prayed. Wept. Rested.

That day didn't give me the answers I sought. But it gave me something better: peace in not knowing and the assurance that Someone still had the map.

Sometimes, life's journey is less about the destination and more about the moments we pause along the way. That foggy morning became a turning point, a reminder that certainty isn't always necessary for progress. It's in the waiting, the listening, and the surrendering that we often find the clarity we've been seeking.

As days turned into weeks, that sense of peace carried me through challenges and uncertainties. I learned to trust the process, to find gratitude in the journey, and to embrace the unknown with an open heart. My work in ministry and writing continued, fueled by a newfound resilience and faith that, regardless of the fog, I was never utterly lost.

In the end, that season taught me an invaluable lesson: sometimes, the clearest vision comes not from seeing the road ahead, but from trusting the One who guides us through the mist. Each step became an act of faith, a testament to the power of belief over sight. I began to notice the beauty in the small things—the way the morning light danced through the fog, how each breath felt like a gift, and the gentle whispers of encouragement that seemed to find me when I least expected them. It was as if the fog itself had become a companion, teaching me to navigate life's uncertainties with grace.

As I shared my experiences with others, I found that many had their own "foggy mornings," moments when clarity seemed elusive and doubt threatened to overshadow hope. Together, we discovered the strength that comes from community, from sharing our stories, and from the collective journey towards understanding and acceptance.

The lessons of that season have stayed with me, reminding me that while the path may not always be clear, the journey is always worthwhile. With each new day, I am reminded to embrace the mysterious and unexpected, to cherish the moments of stillness, and to trust in the greater plan that unfolds beyond my sight.

Scripture Focus: Guiding Light in the Fog

"Your word is a lamp to my feet and a light to my path."

—Psalm 119:105

This verse beautifully illustrates the guidance and clarity that can be found in wisdom and faith. It evokes the image of a traveler navigating through the darkness, where even the smallest light can illuminate the way forward. In life, much like this journey, we often seek direction and understanding, and this passage reminds us of the power of insight and belief to help us find our way. Whether through moments of reflection, meditation, or prayer, we can discover the illumination we need to move confidently toward our goals and aspirations.

"We walk by faith, not by sight."

—2 Corinthians 5:7

This powerful verse reminds us that true belief often requires trusting in things beyond our immediate perception. It encourages us to rely on our inner convictions and the guidance of our hearts, even when the path ahead is uncertain. In life's journey, there are moments when logic and sight may fail us, yet faith empowers us to forge ahead with hope and courage. By embracing this mindset, we open ourselves to new possibilities and the profound understanding that some of the most meaningful aspects of existence are felt rather than seen.

"In returning and rest you shall be saved; in quietness and trust shall be your strength."

—Isaiah 30:15

This passage reminds us of the profound power found in stillness and faith. In a world that often values constant action and noise, it's a gentle call to embrace moments of reflection and trust. By allowing ourselves to pause and rest, we can reconnect with our inner selves and find clarity in the quiet. It's in these moments that strength is truly cultivated, not through force or haste, but through patience and confidence in the journey ahead. Embracing this wisdom can lead to a more balanced and fulfilling life, where peace becomes our guiding force.

Reflect:

- When have you had to walk forward with limited vision?

- What helps you stay grounded when your heart feels unsure?

Prayer & Practice Prompt

Prayer

Lord, I confess that I prefer clarity over trust. I want landmarks, maps, and signposts—but sometimes all You offer is presence. Help me walk by nearness, not by knowledge. Let me remember that You see beyond the fog. And if today all I can do is take one faithful step, let it be enough.

Practice

Take a short walk this week with no destination—just walk and reflect. As you do, consider what it means to move forward without needing to see the whole path. Carry a single verse in your heart and repeat it quietly as you walk.

Pilgrim's Pause

Journaling Prompt:

What do you do when you can't *"feel"* God's nearness? What spiritual practices anchor you when the emotional warmth is gone?

When the sense of divine closeness seems elusive, many find solace in nurturing their faith through various spiritual practices that provide stability and comfort. Engaging in regular prayer or meditation can offer a quiet space to reconnect and reflect, allowing for a deeper understanding of one's spiritual journey. Reading sacred texts or inspirational literature can also provide guidance and remind us of the enduring presence that transcends fleeting emotions.

Additionally, participating in community worship or group discussions can foster a sense of belonging and shared purpose, reinforcing the idea that one is never truly alone in their spiritual quest. Acts of service and kindness can transform feelings of distance into tangible expressions of love and compassion, reminding us of the divine in everyday interactions.

Finally, spending time in nature can be a powerful way to feel connected to something greater than ourselves. The beauty and tranquility of the natural world often serve as a gentle reminder of the presence and creativity of the divine, offering peace and perspective when emotional warmth seems distant.

Group Reflection:

Describe a time when faith looked like showing up, not soaring. How can we encourage each other in the discipline of continuing?

One moment that comes to mind is when a friend was going through a difficult period after losing their job. They felt disheartened and unsure of what the future held. During this time, faith for them wasn't about feeling triumphant or having everything figured out; it was about showing up each day with courage and perseverance, even when it felt challenging.

To encourage each other in the discipline of continuing, we can focus on small, tangible actions. Offering a listening ear, sharing words of encouragement, or simply being present can make a significant difference. Creating a support network where individuals feel seen and valued can help nurture resilience. Setting realistic goals and celebrating small victories can also motivate us to keep moving forward, reminding us that progress often comes in steady, determined steps rather than giant leaps.

2
Shoulders Beneath the Morning

"The Weight of the Yoke"

Charles E. Cravey

The fields awaken in gentle light.

The plow is ready, the furrows deep.

No crowd witnesses the worker's rite.

Yet he strides where few would dare to keep.

With calloused hands and lowered gaze,

He bears the yoke, though no one cheers.

Each step is sacred, a silent praise—

A ritual within the earth so dear.

The harness rubs, the soil holds tight,

The sun climbs high with relentless heat.

Yet Mercy walks where pain takes flight.

And Labor discovers grace beneath its feet.

This is not a race for swifter souls.

Nor a task for those seeking fame.

The One who wore the yoke of old

Still bends to lift what brings us shame.

So onward—though fields stretch far and wide,

Though dust may cling and hearts may break.

The strength lies not in stride or pride.

But in the path you choose to take.

"When the Yoke Feels Heavy but the Heart Grows Strong"

Not all burdens are bad.

Some burdens build you. Shape you. Steady you.

We live in a world where surrender is often mistaken for weakness, and endurance confused with punishment. But Jesus calls weary souls not to escape, but to *exchange*: "Take My yoke upon you...for My yoke is easy, and My burden is light."

Easy? Light?

Not because the path is simple—but because *you no longer carry it alone.*

The yoke, in ancient agrarian life, was a tool of direction and shared effort. Two oxen would walk side-by-side under its weight—one seasoned, the other young. The elder bore most of the load. The younger one learned the rhythm.

That is the yoke Christ offers. He walks beside us. Shoulders the heaviest parts. Teaches us grace in stride and strength in surrender. This isn't toil for toil's sake—it's **training in trust**.

"Let us not grow weary in doing good, for at the proper time we will reap a harvest if we do not give up."

—Galatians 6:9

This timeless verse reminds us of the importance of perseverance and steadfastness in our daily lives. As we navigate through challenges and moments of doubt, it is crucial to hold on to hope and remember that our efforts are not in vain. Each act of kindness, every moment of patience, and every instance of love sown into the world contributes to a greater purpose. The harvest may not be immediate, but it is promised, encouraging us to continue with faith and dedication.

In the quiet moments of reflection, we can find solace in knowing that our journeys are guided by a gentle hand. Embracing each day with renewed determination and a heart full of gratitude transforms mundane tasks into meaningful expressions of devoutness. Let us cherish the path we walk, for it is paved with opportunities to shine light in the lives of others and to grow in grace ourselves.

Daily obedience may look like repetition. But in Heaven's eyes, it looks like love.

So, bear the yoke.

Not with gritted teeth, but with grounded faith. For the One walking beside you is gentle—and strong. And He knows how to bring weary souls home.

Each step, though it may seem small or insignificant, is a testament to your commitment and love. Remember that you are not alone on this path; there is a divine presence accompanying you, offering strength and guidance. As you bear your burdens, do so with the understanding that they are shaping you, molding you into a beacon of light for others.

Each trial is an opportunity to deepen your faith and expand your capacity for compassion. Trust in the process and in the gentle whispers of encouragement that remind you of your purpose. In moments of weariness, pause to reflect on the beauty of the journey and the growth it fosters. Allow yourself to be anchored in hope, knowing that each act of obedience is a step toward the fulfillment of a greater promise.

A Pilgrim's Glimpse: Lessons in the Furrow

I once watched an old farmer at the edge of a cornfield, just after dawn. I'd pulled over on a country road to make a call, but the sight made me pause.

He was alone, guiding a rust-stained tractor through rows he must've plowed a thousand times. No audience. No applause. Just dirt, diesel, and the rhythm of resolve.

I sat there longer than I intended.

The furrows were as straight as sermons. His pace never hurried. His back never arched in complaint. There was something reverent about it—not just work, but worship.

I remember thinking, *this is what faithfulness looks like when no one's watching.*

It wasn't flashy. It wasn't new. But it was necessary.

So many days in ministry and life feel like that tractor's path—repetition without recognition. But the field remembers. The fruit remembers. And most of all, God remembers.

I drove off with an odd sense of comfort: maybe I don't have to change the world in a day. Maybe I just need to keep showing up in the field I've been given.

Scripture Focus: Bearing the Easy Yoke

"Come to Me, all you who are weary and burdened, and I will give you rest.

Take My yoke upon you and learn from Me, for I am gentle and humble in heart,

and you will find rest for your souls. For My yoke is easy and My burden is light."

—Matthew 11:28–30

This invitation isn't just for the broken; it's for the consistent—the souls who have shown up day after day with blistered hands and bowed shoulders. Christ doesn't remove all weight. He invites us to carry **with** Him. And in that shared rhythm, we find rest—not escape, but holy endurance.

In this sacred partnership, we discover a profound sense of peace and purpose. It is a call to embrace a journey that, while challenging, is marked by companionship and divine support. Each step taken under the shared yoke becomes an opportunity to grow in resilience and grace.

As we walk alongside, we learn to listen deeply, to trust more fully, and to love more generously. This invitation extends beyond mere relief; it is a transformative experience that nurtures the spirit and renews the heart. Thus, the weary find solace, not in the absence of trials, but in the presence of unwavering love and unyielding hope.

May we accept this invitation, not as a temporary reprieve, but as a lifelong promise of strength and serenity, guiding us through every season of life with faith and courage.

"It is good for a man to bear the yoke while he is young.

Let him sit alone in silence, for the Lord has laid it on him."

—Lamentations 3:27–28

There is no shame in silence. The early yoke isn't punishment—it's **preparation**. Seasons of quiet obedience form the muscles of spiritual maturity.

In these moments of reflection, we learn patience and resilience, developing a deeper understanding of ourselves and our purpose. Just as a seed must rest in the darkness before it can sprout, so too must we embrace periods of solitude to grow and flourish. These times teach us to listen, to be still, and to appreciate the gentle whispers of wisdom that often go unheard amidst the noise of daily life.

As we carry this yoke, we are reminded that it is not a burden destined to weigh us down, but rather a tool to cultivate strength and grace. Through it, we gain the ability to face challenges with a steady heart and a grounded spirit. This preparation equips us to navigate the complexities of life with humility and compassion, as we are molded into vessels of service and love.

In the sacred silence, we find clarity and purpose, emerging with renewed faith and a readiness to embrace the path that lies ahead, knowing that every step has been guided by a hand that seeks our ultimate good.

"Whatever you do, work heartily, as for the Lord and not for men."

—**Colossians 3:23**

When recognition fades and effort feels unnoticed, remember: Heaven sees every faithful furrow.

Each moment of dedication and every sincere intention are valued beyond earthly measures. In times when you feel that your labor goes unseen, hold onto the assurance that your work contributes to a greater purpose. Your perseverance and integrity light the path for others, inspiring them to follow suit. Embrace the joy found in doing your best, knowing that it is cherished and celebrated in ways that transcend human accolades. Let this perspective be your guiding star, reminding you that true fulfillment comes from within and from the divine recognition of a life well-lived.

Prayer & Practice Prompt

Prayer

Lord, I confess I've sometimes seen obedience as a burden instead of an invitation. I've strained against the weight, forgetting that You shoulder it with me. Teach me to walk at Your pace. To find joy in the mundane. And to believe that the field You've placed me in is holy ground.

Amen.

Practice

Choose one small task this week and do it **as worship**—not for praise, not for efficiency, but as a sacred offering. Whether it's folding laundry, writing in solitude, or tending a relationship, carry it like a yoke—with Christ walking beside you.

Pilgrim's Pause

Journaling Prompt:

What task in your life right now feels repetitive or unappreciated? How might it look different if you imagined Christ yoked beside you?

Reflecting on this prompt, I find that the daily chore of tidying up my living space often feels repetitive and underappreciated. Each day, I pick up scattered items, dust surfaces, and organize belongings, only to find myself repeating the same tasks the next day.

However, if I imagine Christ yoked beside me, this routine transforms into a meaningful act of service and mindfulness. With His presence, each movement becomes a conscious, gentle expression of care and gratitude for the space I inhabit. His companionship brings a sense of purpose and joy, reminding me that even in mundane tasks, there is an opportunity for connection and growth. The act of cleaning becomes not just an obligation but a moment to reflect on simplicity and grace, infusing the ordinary with divine significance.

Group Reflection:

How can we encourage one another in the long obedience of the everyday? Share a time when the unseen labor bore visible fruit much later.

It's important to remember that small, consistent efforts often lead to meaningful outcomes over time. Encouragement can come in many forms, such as offering words of affirmation, sharing personal stories of perseverance, or simply being present and listening when someone needs support.

One example of unseen labor bearing fruit is the story of a teacher who spent years mentoring and inspiring students. Initially, it seemed like just another routine part of their job, but over time, the impact became evident as former students returned to express how those lessons and encouragement had shaped their lives and careers. This demonstrates that even when progress isn't immediately visible, the seeds we plant today can grow into something beautiful and significant in the future.

Encouraging each other in our daily efforts means recognizing and celebrating these small victories, understanding that they contribute to a greater tapestry of achievement and fulfillment.

3

The Fellowship of the Furnace

"When You Walk Through Fire…"

"In the Heart of the Fire"

Charles E. Cravey

The flames leapt high, the smoke billowed thick,
The ground below began to moan—
Yet amidst the fiercest blaze,
I discovered I was not alone.

The world had cast its threats like shackles.
With fury cloaked in royal pride,
Though they sought to bind me to the flames,
A Greater Presence walked inside.

I did not perceive His robe or face.
No thunder spoke, no wind replied—
But in the stillness, grace abounded.
And peace that fire could not divide.

Let tyrants forge their golden idols,
Let trials come with smoke and sting—
If in the blaze I walk with God,
I fear not what the fire may bring.

Devotional Reflection: The Furnace Is Not the End

Fire rarely asks permission.

It consumes what it touches, distills what it can't destroy, and tests the truth of what remains. And for those walking in faith, it often shows up uninvited.

Scripture doesn't hide this. In fact, it leans into it:

"Beloved, do not be surprised at the fiery trial… as though something strange were happening to you." (1 Peter 4:12)

Daniel's friends didn't flinch at the fire. They didn't beg to be spared from it—they only resolved to stand. And when the flames came, they stepped in with the quiet defiance of trust.

Because they believed this: God doesn't always deliver *from* the furnace, but He never **fails** to join us *in* it.

Sometimes, His greatest work isn't in rescue—**it's in refinement**.

The fire melts away what was never meant to last. Fear. Pretenses. Pride. What's left is gold—tested, real, radiant.

"I have refined you, but not as silver; I have tried you in the furnace of affliction."

—Isaiah 48:10

Your affliction is not your identity. The fire is not forever. But what God forges in you there **is**.

So, when you find yourself amid the flames, remember that it is not a sign of abandonment, but of transformation. Like a potter with clay, God shapes us through the heat of our trials, crafting something beautiful and enduring.

Hold fast to hope, for the furnace can be a place of profound growth and revelation. It is where faith is purified and strengthened, where reliance on divine strength becomes essential. In these moments, the presence of God is not just a comfort; it is a promise that you are never alone.

As you face your own fiery trials, take courage from those who walked before you, their stories etched in the tapestry of faith. Let their resilience inspire you, their victories remind you that the flames do not have the final word.

And let love be your guide through the heat. Love for others, love for yourself, and love for the One who walks with you through every blaze. For in the end, it is love that endures, shining brighter than any flame, a beacon of hope and renewal.

Remember, the furnace is not the end—it is the beginning of a new chapter, a testament to the strength and beauty that emerge when faith is tested and refined.

A Pilgrim's Glimpse: The Night the Church Burned

Years ago, I received a call no pastor wants. An African American church near me had been burned to the ground. By the time I arrived the following morning, it was mostly smoke and smoldering beams. The sanctuary where voices had lifted for decades was blackened. Charred Bibles. Fallen rafters. Memories undone in minutes.

I stood in the ashes and wept—not just for the loss, but for the sheer finality of it. There was no sanctuary left. Just dust, embers, and questions.

But what happened next was resurrection.

The congregation of that church didn't scatter. They circled. Prayed. Planned. They worshiped in borrowed spaces—cafeterias, tents, and one Sunday under a shade tree. People gave more generously than ever.

The fire had taken the structure, but it couldn't touch the spirit.

In time, the church rebuilt—not just a sanctuary, but our understanding of what the Church truly is. Not walls, not windows. But presence. Fellowship. Flame-born faith.

Sometimes it takes fire to remind us of where the real altar stands.

Scripture Focus: Presence in the Flame

"When you walk through the fire, you shall not be burned, and the flame shall not consume you."

—Isaiah 43:2

Even when smoke blinds our view, He walks unfazed beside us.

His presence is a beacon of hope, guiding us through the thickest darkness and the fiercest storms. We find strength in His unwavering support, as He whispers words of comfort and encouragement into our hearts. With each step we take, we are reminded that we are never alone; a divine hand holds ours, lifting us up when we falter and carrying us when our burdens feel too heavy. The challenges we face become less daunting, for we know that with faith, resilience, and His eternal love, we can overcome anything.

"So Shadrach, Meshach, and Abednego came out of the fire... and there was no smell of fire on them."

—**Daniel 3:26–27**

Deliverance doesn't always mean detour. Sometimes it means *walking through without being destroyed.* It's about emerging on the other side, refined and resilient, carrying with you newfound strength and wisdom. Life's challenges can be intense, like a crucible, but they can also forge a greater understanding and appreciation for the journey itself. Just as the three men emerged unscathed, our own trials can be opportunities for growth, teaching us the power of faith, perseverance, and the support of a loving community. It's a reminder that even when the path is daunting, we are not alone, and we can find hope and courage to face whatever lies ahead with grace and determination.

"In this you rejoice, though now for a little while, if necessary, you have been grieved by various trials... so that the tested genuineness of your faith—more precious than gold—may result in praise..."

—**1 Peter 1:6–7**

Faith forged in fire carries a weight that cannot be shaken.

It stands resilient, a beacon of strength and hope in times of adversity. Each challenge faced and overcome adds another layer of depth and understanding, a testament to the unwavering spirit within. This faith, tempered by trials, shines brightly in the darkest of times, offering warmth and guidance not only to the one who bears it but also to those around them. It becomes a source of inspiration, reminding us all that through perseverance and belief, we can emerge stronger and more compassionate, ready to embrace life's journey with courage and grace.

Prayer & Practice Prompt

Prayer

Lord, the fire frightens me. I confess—I want comfort over refining. But I know You are the God **in the fire,** not just around it. So, walk with me. Burn away what holds me back. Leave only what reflects You. Amen.

Practice

This week, name a trial you've faced—or are still facing. Write out what it took, what it taught, and where you saw God in it. If you're comfortable, share it with someone else who might be walking through their own furnace.

Pilgrim's Pause

Journaling Prompt:

What "furnace" has marked your life? What good came from the refining—even if it didn't come right away?

When I think about the "furnace" that has marked my life, my thoughts inevitably turn to the challenging period during my transition to a new city for work. It was a time filled with uncertainty and loneliness, as I left behind family, friends, and the familiar comforts of home. The days felt long and daunting, like being thrust into an intense heat that seemed unending.

Yet, from this experience emerged profound personal growth and resilience. I learned the invaluable skill of self-reliance, discovering strengths I never knew I possessed. This period of trial taught me the importance of cultivating new relationships, leading to friendships that have enriched my life in unexpected ways. It also prompted me to explore new hobbies and interests, expanding my horizons beyond what I had previously imagined.

Over time, the lessons from this furnace of change turned into a source of confidence and empowerment. I found that each small victory—whether successfully navigating a new environment or overcoming a moment of doubt—contributed to a newfound sense of purpose and fulfillment. It reminded me that even amid life's most intense heat, there can be beauty and transformation, shaping us into stronger, more compassionate versions of ourselves.

Group Reflection:

Why do you think God sometimes chooses to walk with us **in** the fire instead of removing us **from** it?

It is often said that facing challenges head-on can lead to profound growth and transformation. Walking through the fire, rather than being removed from it, can strengthen our resilience and deepen our understanding of ourselves and our faith. Such experiences may teach us important lessons about perseverance, trust, and the power of community. When we are in the fire, we may also become more empathetic and compassionate towards others who are facing similar trials. This journey can help us find inner strength and discover that we are never truly alone, as divine presence and support are with us every step of the way.

4

Grace at the Gate

"While he was still a long way off..."

"The Gate That Waited"

Charles E. Cravey

I thought the gate would groan and close.

When I returned with shame in tow.

I feared the lock, the wrath, the rose.

That withered long ago.

But there it stood with hinges wide,

No scorn upon the weathered stone.

No guards to jeer, no rules to hide—

Just welcome carved in wood alone.

A Father ran without demand.

With robe and ring and tear-streaked face.

He did not ask where I had been—

He only pulled me into grace.

So, if you wander, bruise, or break,

And dread the threshold you must meet—

Take heart, dear soul. The gates don't shake

When grace has nailed them at His feet.

Devotional Reflection: The Arms That Found Me First

The prodigal story doesn't begin with speech—it begins with **sight**.

"While he was still a long way off, his father saw him..." (Luke 15:20). Before the apology. Before the explanation. Grace had already started running.

This is the mystery of mercy. It meets you at the edge. Not with interrogation but embrace.

We often imagine God's threshold like a courtroom. But in truth, it's more *like a porch light left on*, a robe held ready, a meal half-prepared in hope.

Grace is not leniency—it's lavishness. It isn't a pass—it's a place to rest. And it comes not when we've made ourselves worthy, but precisely when we're most aware that we're not.

"Let us then come boldly to the throne of grace…" (Hebrews 4:16)

Not cautiously. Not with disclaimers. **Boldly**—because Christ already bore the shame.

The pilgrim's journey doesn't end in perfection. It ends in **welcome**. It ends at the open arms of a love that knows no bounds. This journey is not marked by the steps we take alone, but by the steps that are met with divine companionship. Each misstep is not a cause for rejection but an opportunity for redemption. In the quiet of the heart, where fears and doubts often dwell, grace whispers a gentle invitation: "Come as you are."

The path may be winding and sometimes shadowed by uncertainty, but it is never without light. The light of grace guides us, illuminating the way forward, reminding us that our worth is not determined by our failures but by the infinite love that calls us home. It is a journey that transforms, reshaping our understanding of what it means to be truly seen and truly loved.

And so, we walk on, not towards judgment, but towards a celebration. A feast where everyone is welcome, where every heart is known, and where love is the language spoken. The prodigal story, then, is not just about returning; it is about arriving, about finding that home has been waiting for us all along.

A Pilgrim's Glimpse: The Time I Almost Didn't Go In

There was a season when I stopped going to church.

I still believed. Still prayed. But I felt like a failure. I was burned out, discouraged, and unsure of where I fit. I thought, "Why show up when you feel like a mess?"

One Sunday, I sat in the parking lot for fifteen minutes, engine running. Debated going home. But something—someone—nudged me in.

No lightning bolt. No spectacular moment. Just a handshake at the door, a familiar song, a whispered reminder during prayer: "You're still mine."

That's the miracle of grace. It doesn't wait for us to clean up. It meets us in the parking lot.

That Sunday, I didn't walk into church a shining saint. I walked in as a limping pilgrim. And it was enough.

Scripture Focus: Gates That Swing on Grace

"Lift up your heads, O gates! Be lifted up, you ancient doors, that the King of glory may come in."

—Psalm 24:7

Grace doesn't sneak in. It enters **glory first**. It strides boldly, illuminating the darkest corners of the human heart with its radiant light. Grace transforms everything it touches, leaving a trail of hope and renewal in its wake. With a gentle power, it invites us to open our hearts and embrace the possibilities of redemption and change. It reminds us that we are never alone, for the King of Glory stands at the threshold, ready to fill our lives with love and purpose.

"I am the gate. Whoever enters through Me will be saved. They will come in and go out and find pasture."

—John 10:9

The gate is not guarded by shame. The Shepherd opens it. The path beyond is filled with light and promise, a sanctuary for weary souls seeking solace and renewal. Here, the Shepherd guides each step with care, ensuring that every journey is met with understanding and love. The pasture is lush and abundant, a testament to the Shepherd's unwavering commitment to provision and peace. In this sacred space, fear dissipates, replaced by a profound sense of belonging and grace.

"Therefore, there is now no condemnation for those who are in Christ Jesus..."

—Romans 8:1

Even when the accuser speaks, grace answers louder. In the quiet moments when doubt creeps in and the whispers of inadequacy try to take hold, remember that grace stands unwavering. It is a gentle yet powerful force, embracing and uplifting, reminding us of our inherent worth and the love that surrounds us.

Grace is not just a concept but a living, breathing presence that reassures and renews, no matter the circumstances. It invites us to step into the light of a new day with confidence and hope, knowing that our past does not define us and our future is rich with promise.

Prayer & Practice Prompt

Prayer

Lord, I hesitate at thresholds. I rehearse my failures more than Your mercy. But today, I dare to step closer—not because I am worthy, but because You said, Come. Thank You for a gate that swings wide with love. Amen.

Practice

This week, extend grace to someone who may expect rejection. A phone call, a note, a gesture. In doing so, you become part of the "gate ministry"—the welcome of God with skin on.

Pilgrim's Pause

Journaling Prompt:

Where in your life have you hesitated to receive grace? What might it look like to walk through the gate anyway?

Perhaps in times when you've felt undeserving of kindness, you might have hesitated to receive grace. It could be moments when mistakes loomed large, and the weight of self-judgment made acceptance difficult. Walking through the gate of grace might look like gently setting aside your inner critic, allowing compassion to take its place. It could mean embracing forgiveness—not just from others, but from yourself—recognizing that growth often requires vulnerability. Picture yourself stepping forward with an open heart, ready to accept the warmth and understanding that grace offers, knowing that it can be a powerful catalyst for healing and transformation.

Group Reflection:

How can communities of faith better reflect the posture of the Father—watchful, open-armed, quick to run?

In fostering a spirit of inclusion and compassion, communities of faith can draw inspiration from the Father's loving nature by actively engaging in practices that demonstrate genuine care and acceptance. This involves creating a welcoming environment where everyone feels valued and heard. By listening intently to the needs and stories of others, communities can better understand and respond to the unique challenges faced by individuals.

Moreover, actively reaching out to those on the margins and extending support without hesitation mirrors the Father's readiness to run towards those in need. This can be achieved through community service projects, support groups, and initiatives that address both physical and spiritual needs. Providing spaces for open dialogue and learning can also encourage growth and understanding among members, fostering a deeper sense of unity and purpose.

By embodying these qualities, communities of faith can become beacons of hope and love, reflecting the Father's embrace in a world yearning for connection and compassion.

5

Ashes Beneath the Altar

"Offer your bodies as a living sacrifice..."

"Smoke That Rises Still"

Charles E. Cravey

I brought no gold, no flawless prize—

Just remnants charred by seasons long.

Yet still the smoke began to rise,

As weakness rose in sacred song.

Upon the altar, ash and flame,

A broken heart, a silent cry.

I offered all and named His name,

And watched my lesser kingdoms die.

The fire consumed, but not in wrath,

It burned away what weighed me down.

And left behind a clearer path—

A crown exchanged for mercy's crown.

So now I kneel where smoke has been,

And find the place of yielding sweet.

For even ashes speak of Him—

Still holy, where surrender meets.

Devotional Reflection: When Letting Go Becomes Worship

There comes a moment in every journey when something must be **laid down**.

A dream. A plan. A version of yourself. Something precious, or perhaps just familiar. And when you lay it on the altar—not with resignation, but reverence—it becomes "worship."

In the Old Testament, sacrifice was fragrant to God not because of the perfection of the offering but because of the posture of the one who gave it. The ashes beneath the altar were not signs of loss—they were testimonies of trust.

Romans 12:1 calls us to offer ourselves as "living sacrifices"—not one-time flames, but daily incense. We don't just lay down what's easy; we surrender what we cling to. And the fire? It purifies.

"Unless a grain of wheat falls to the ground and dies, it remains alone..." (John 12:24)

There is a kind of dying that leads to deeper living.

What you offer may feel small. But once offered, it becomes sacred.

It is transformed through the act of surrender, becoming a part of something greater than itself. This sacred exchange invites us into a deeper relationship with the Divine, where every relinquished dream or plan is met with grace and renewal.

In letting go, we create space for new growth and possibilities. Just as a gardener prunes away the old to encourage fresh blooms, we too must sometimes release what no longer serves us to make room for what is yet to come.

This act of worship is not about loss but about trust—trust in the unseen, trust in the process, and trust in the promise of new beginnings. It is an acknowledgment that there is beauty in the unknown and that faith can turn the act of letting go into a profound expression of love and devotion.

So, as you lay down whatever burdens your heart, do so with the assurance that you are stepping into a sacred dance of renewal. Each step, each surrender, brings you closer to the heart of the Divine, where the ashes of what you let go are transformed into the fertile soil of a life lived fully in faith.

A Pilgrim's Glimpse: The Manuscript I Buried

Years ago, I spent months working on a manuscript I believed would be ***the*** turning point in my writing. I poured vision, late nights, and prayer into it. And just as it neared completion, I sensed a quiet conviction: ***Lay it down.***

Everything in me resisted. Surely that couldn't be the Spirit—not after all this effort? But the tug remained.

So, I shelved it. Didn't finish it. Didn't pitch it. I set it before the Lord and said, "If You want it, it's Yours."

It felt like death.

But in the quiet afterward, space opened. My mind cleared. New words came—**better** words. A new project arose that touched far more lives than I ever imagined.

That shelved manuscript wasn't wasted. It was a seed that had to fall and die.

Some sacrifices aren't lost. They're just buried in holy ground.

And over time, they transform in ways we can't initially comprehend. The lessons learned from that manuscript guided me in unexpected directions, enriching my journey as a writer.

Every now and then, I revisit the dusty corner where the manuscript rests, a gentle reminder of the path I've traveled. It serves as a testament to the mysterious ways creativity and faith intertwine.

I've come to understand that sometimes, letting go is the most profound act of creation. It allows for growth, for new visions to emerge, and for the unexpected to take root in the fertile soil of possibility.

In the end, what matters is not just the story we tell, but the journey we embrace along the way—the journey that shapes us and the stories that find us when we're ready to listen.

Scripture Focus: Surrender as Sacred Flame

"Therefore, I urge you... offer your bodies as a living sacrifice, holy and pleasing to God..."

—Romans 12:1

Worship isn't always loud. Sometimes it's what we let go of when no one sees.

It's in the quiet moments of reflection where true devotion often takes root. In the stillness, we find the strength to release our burdens and embrace the transformative power of faith.

This kind of worship is deeply personal, a sacred exchange between the heart and the divine. It requires courage to surrender, to trust in the unseen, and to believe that our offerings, no matter how small, are cherished and meaningful.

As we navigate the complexities of life, let us remember that our silent acts of faith can speak volumes, creating ripples of grace and love that touch the world in profound and unexpected ways.

"Even though the fig tree does not bud... I will rejoice in the Lord..."

—Habakkuk 3:17–18

Faith doesn't require visible fruit to offer praise.

It finds its strength in the unseen, trusting in the steadfastness of promises yet to be fulfilled. This unwavering hope is a testament to resilience, a beacon that shines even in the darkest of times. Like a seed planted in the depths of winter, faith knows that the warmth of spring will eventually come, bringing with it life and abundance.

In moments of uncertainty, when the world seems barren and the future unclear, faith whispers a gentle reminder to hold fast. It encourages a heart to sing even when circumstances suggest silence, to dance in the rain of adversity, and to celebrate the unseen victories that lie ahead. For in faith, there is a profound understanding that blessings may not always be immediate or obvious, but they are present nonetheless, waiting to unfold in their perfect time.

Thus, faith becomes a sacred journey, an inner pilgrimage where the soul finds peace and joy not in the external, but in the eternal. It is a call to trust in the divine tapestry being woven, one that is full of mystery and grace, inviting us to rejoice in the journey itself, knowing we are never alone.

"He will sit as a refiner and purifier of silver..."

—Malachi 3:3

The heat that refines isn't wrath—it's love in flame.

It's the kind of love that sees potential beyond the impurities, a love that patiently endures the fire to bring forth brilliance. In the crucible of life, challenges and trials become the tools of transformation. Just as the silversmith carefully monitors the temperature, never leaving the metal unattended, so too does this divine love watch over us, ensuring that we are never tested beyond our strength.

In this process, imperfections rise to the surface to be gently removed, revealing the true essence of what lies beneath. It's a journey of becoming, where the heart is polished to reflect the light that it was always meant to shine. And in this sacred act of refining, we find not only beauty but also strength, resilience, and a deeper understanding of who we are meant to be.

Thus, through the metaphor of the silver and the silversmith, we are reminded of the transformative power of love—a force that purifies, not by destruction, but by nurturing the very best within us.

Prayer & Practice Prompt

Prayer

Father, I bring what I've held tightly. My plans. My pride. My place. If You ask for it, I will lay it down. Teach me that ashes can still rise in worship. And that what dies in obedience lives in glory. Amen.

Practice

Find a quiet moment this week. Light a candle or sit near a fire. Reflect on something you've been reluctant to surrender. Then, in prayer, offer it—not as a loss, but as a sacred gift. Name it. Trust it to God.

Pilgrim's Pause

Journaling Prompt:

What have you laid down in this season—or what might God be asking of you? How can you view it not as defeat, but as devotion?

Taking time to reflect on the changes in this season, I realize that laying something down isn't necessarily about loss; it's about creating space for growth and new opportunities. Perhaps God is asking me to release my grip on the need for control, to trust in the unfolding of life with faith and patience.

By viewing this act of letting go as a form of devotion, I can embrace it as an offering of my trust and love. It becomes an opportunity to deepen my spiritual journey, to cultivate resilience, and to open my heart to the unknown with grace and courage. In this way, what I lay down transforms into a sacred act of surrender, allowing me to walk forward with renewed purpose and hope.

Group Reflection:

Discuss a time when something surrendered led to unexpected growth. What was born from the ashes?

The experience that comes to mind for me is when our team had to let go of a long-standing project that we had invested a lot of time and effort into. Initially, it felt like a significant loss, but surrendering it opened up new opportunities for us.

From the ashes of that project, a fresh and innovative idea emerged that aligned more closely with our evolving goals. We began to focus on developing a new platform that not only met the needs of our audience more effectively but also sparked creativity within our team. This shift allowed us to explore new technologies and collaborate in ways we hadn't considered before.

The unexpected growth that followed was not just in our product but also in our team dynamics. We learned to communicate better, embrace change with optimism, and remain resilient in the face of setbacks. By letting go of what no longer served us, we cultivated a renewed sense of purpose and enthusiasm that propelled us forward, turning what seemed like an ending into a promising new beginning.

6
The Stream Beside the Struggle

"You prepare a table before me in the presence of my enemies..."

Water for the Weary

Charles E. Cravey

I did not leave the storm behind—

It still rolled on, with wind and wave.

Yet at my feet, a stream I find,

That whispers peace and makes me brave.

The thunder groans, the sky hangs low,

My path is rough, my strength unsure.

But still the waters gently flow,

A grace that steadies, soft and pure.

I drink, not free from toil or pain,

But drawn by comfort just the same.

For even here, amid the strain,

There runs a mercy none can name.

So let the storm above me stay—

I've found a peace no winds can steal.

A stream that sings beneath dismay,

And fills my soul with quiet zeal.

Devotional Reflection: Peace That Doesn't Wait

Most people imagine peace as something that *arrives after the battle is over*. But Scripture paints a richer picture.

"You prepare a table before me in the presence of my enemies..." (Psalm 23:5)

Not after. *In the presence of.*

That's the kind of peace only God can give—a peace that sits down in the middle of chaos and quietly says, "I'm not going anywhere."

The world teaches you to strive for serenity by removing pressure. But the Spirit speaks in paradox: *You are seen, held, and nourished even while the waves rise.* Peace doesn't wait. It walks beside. It pours from a stream most miss because they're chasing a finish line.

"The peace of God, which surpasses all understanding, will guard your hearts..." (Philippians 4:7)

God's peace doesn't ask permission from your circumstances. It simply comes—and stays.

It settles into the deepest corners of your soul, offering a serene refuge amidst life's storms. This peace whispers gently in moments of doubt, reminding you that you are never alone. It is a steadfast companion, unwavering in its presence, even when the world around you feels chaotic and unpredictable.

In this divine tranquility, you find the strength to face challenges with grace and courage. It empowers you to let go of worries that weigh you down and encourages you to embrace each day with a hopeful heart. As you lean into this peace, you discover a profound sense of contentment, knowing that you are held and cherished by a love greater than any earthly trouble.

So, when life feels overwhelming, remember to pause and breathe in the peace that surpasses all understanding. Let it fill you with calm assurance, guiding you gently through every trial and triumph.

A Pilgrim's Glimpse: Porch Coffee in a Storm

There was a day I remember vividly—rain hammering the rooftop, thunder muttering like distant giants.

I had nothing fixed, nothing solved. Bills due. A deadline missed. A long silence from someone I loved.

And yet... I sat on the porch, coffee in hand, and exhaled.

Not because the storm ended, but because somehow, God showed up in that rocking chair with me. No answers. Just presence.

The warmth of the cup. The rhythm of rain. A scripture in my heart. "The Lord is near."

That moment didn't fix my world. But it flooded my soul with stillness. And that was enough to keep going.

Scripture Focus: Peace in the Middle of It

"You will keep in perfect peace those whose minds are steadfast, because they trust in You."

—Isaiah 26:3

Peace is not the absence of struggle. It's the presence of trust.

When we place our faith in something greater than ourselves, we find a serene stability amid life's storms. This peace does not come from avoiding challenges but from embracing them with confidence in our ability to overcome. Trust acts as an anchor, grounding us when the waves of uncertainty crash against our shores. By nurturing a steadfast mind and an open heart, we cultivate a sanctuary within ourselves where tranquility resides, allowing us to navigate each day with grace and resilience.

"Do not be anxious... but in every situation, by prayer and petition, with thanksgiving, present your requests to God."

—Philippians 4:6

Prayer opens the gate where peace flows in. It acts as a soothing balm for the restless mind, offering comfort and clarity in times of uncertainty. When we take a moment to pause, breathe, and communicate with the divine, we invite serenity into our hearts. This practice of connecting with a higher power reminds us that we are not alone and that our burdens can be shared and lightened.

In the quiet moments of reflection, we find strength and courage to face the challenges that lie ahead. Through prayer, we cultivate a spirit of gratitude, acknowledging the blessings in our lives and the lessons learned from our struggles. It encourages us to focus on the positive, fostering a mindset of hope and resilience.

As we continue on our journey, let us remember the power of prayer to transform our worries into peace and our fears into faith. In every situation, may we find solace and inspiration in the simple act of reaching out, knowing that each whisper of prayer is heard and cherished.

"They will drink from the river of Your delights."

—Psalm 36:8

This river never runs dry. It flows eternally, offering sustenance and joy to all who seek its waters. Its currents are gentle yet profound, carrying with them a promise of renewal and hope. Those who come to this river find solace in its depths, where worries are washed away and spirits are uplifted.

The landscape surrounding the river is lush and vibrant, teeming with life and color. Trees stretch their branches towards the sky, their leaves whispering secrets in the breeze. Flowers bloom in a riot of hues, painting the ground with their beauty, while birds sing melodious tunes, creating a symphony of nature that soothes the heart.

In this serene setting, time seems to stand still, allowing moments of reflection and gratitude. The river invites all to pause and savor the simple joys of life, reminding us of the abundance that flows from a source of divine love. Here, amidst the gentle ripples and the tranquil ambiance, one finds a deep connection to the world and a sense of peace that transcends understanding.

Prayer & Practice Prompt

Prayer

Lord, I don't ask You to always stop the storm—only to remind me You're beside me in it. Help me notice the quiet stream while the thunder still rolls. Let Your peace guard my heart more fiercely than any outcome ever could. Amen.

Practice

Take time this week to sit somewhere still—even just 10 minutes. No phone. No task. Just breathe, listen, and invite God into the moment. Let that quiet become the stream that sustains you.

Pilgrim's Pause

Journaling Prompt:

When have you experienced peace that didn't match your circumstances? What anchored you in that moment?

I recall a time when life felt particularly tumultuous—a whirlwind of responsibilities, deadlines, and unexpected challenges. Yet, amidst the chaos, I found myself sitting quietly in a small park during my lunch break. The world seemed to pause around me as I focused on the gentle rustle of leaves in the breeze, the distant laughter of children playing, and the warmth of the sun on my face. It was as if I had entered a different realm where time slowed down, and tranquility enveloped me.

What anchored me in that moment was the simple act of being present. I allowed myself to fully engage with the sensory experiences around me, letting go of worries and future plans. The grounding presence of nature reminded me of the beauty and continuity of life, even when things felt uncertain. This peace, though contrasting sharply with my circumstances, felt deeply reassuring, a reminder that serenity can always be found within, regardless of external chaos.

Group Reflection:

How can we help one another recognize and rest beside the stream—***before*** the storm is over?

What happens when we become overwhelmed by the demands of life? One way is to cultivate a culture of mindfulness and presence within our group. By encouraging regular check-ins and creating safe spaces for open communication, we can support each other in identifying when stress begins to build.

Additionally, we can share practices that promote relaxation and grounding, such as meditation, deep breathing, or nature walks. These activities can serve as gentle reminders to pause and find calm amid chaos.

Finally, expressing empathy and understanding towards one another's struggles can foster a sense of community and resilience. By being present for each other and offering a listening ear or a compassionate word, we create an environment where everyone feels supported and valued, making it easier to find moments of peace even before the storm has passed.

7
The Wound That Worshiped

"Blessed are those who mourn..."

"The Altar in My Ache"

Charles E. Cravey

I brought my ache to holy ground,

Not wrapped in strength, not stitched in pride —

But open, raw, and still unbound,

A hurt too heavy still to hide.

I did not wait to feel restored,

Or speak in hymns I could not claim.

I knelt where grief and grace outpoured—

And wept my way into His name.

He did not flinch. He did not flee.

He sat with me and touched the bruise.

And in that wound, He gave to me

A healing I could never lose.

So now I bring the broken praise—

A song that limps, a hallelujah scar.

And I have found in all my days:

The altar's never very far.

Devotional Reflection: Scars That Still Sing

There's a kind of worship that doesn't come from the mountaintop—but from the floor of the valley.

The kind that's not well-rehearsed. It's breathtaking. Tear-streaked. Sometimes wordless. But it's holy.

David knew this. He cried, **"My tears have been my food day and night..." (Psalm 42:3).** And yet he still whispered hope. Still showed up at the altar. Still sang.

In this world that prizes polish and performance, it's easy to think God wants tidy faith. But Scripture tells a different story: **"A bruised reed He will not break, and a smoldering wick He will not snuff out" (Isaiah 42:3).**

Your pain is not a disqualifier—it's an offering.

There are songs only sorrow can write. Prayers only pain can birth. And there's a kind of worship that—though cracked and trembling—shines all the brighter because of it.

"My sacrifice, O God, is a broken spirit; a broken and contrite heart You, God, will not despise."

—Psalm 51:17

Even your wound can worship. And sometimes... it worships best.

When we approach with our vulnerabilities laid bare, we allow ourselves to be truly seen and understood. In these moments, our authenticity shines through, creating a profound connection with the divine. It's in the rawness of our pain and the honesty of our struggles that our worship becomes most genuine.

This kind of worship doesn't require eloquent words or grand gestures. Instead, it speaks through the quiet surrender of our hearts, the willingness to admit our need for healing and grace. It is an offering of our true selves, in all our brokenness and beauty.

As we acknowledge our wounds, we invite healing and transformation. It is here, in the midst of our imperfection, that we find the strength to rise, renewed and filled with hope. Our brokenness becomes a bridge, leading us to deeper compassion and understanding, both for ourselves and for others.

In this sacred space, we discover that our wounds are not a barrier to divine love but a pathway to experiencing it more fully. We learn that even in our frailty, we are held, cherished, and embraced by a love that knows no bounds.

A Pilgrim's Glimpse: The Day I Led Through Tears

I once had to lead prayer the morning after devastating personal news. Everything in me wanted to call someone else. Stay home. Go silent.

But I felt a still whisper: "Come anyway."

I remember standing in front of the congregation, trembling. Voice thin. Eyes swollen.

And then—halfway through—I stopped praying *for* them and started praying **with** them. My voice cracked. My hands shook. But what came out wasn't hollow.

It was real.

And I watched something happen—not just in me, but in them. Walls fell. Tears flowed. Masks lifted.

That wasn't the cleanest prayer I've ever prayed.

But I think it might've been the most honest one.

Scripture Focus: The God Who Sees the Broken

"He heals the brokenhearted and binds up their wounds."

—Psalm 147:3

Healing isn't always immediate. But it always begins with being seen. Being seen allows us to feel acknowledged and understood, providing a foundation for the healing journey. It reminds us that we are not alone in our struggles and that there is hope for renewal. This recognition can come from a caring friend, a compassionate stranger, or even from within us as we learn to accept and forgive our own imperfections.

The process of healing is unique for everyone. It may involve self-reflection, seeking support, or finding solace in spiritual practices. It often requires patience, as we gradually piece together the parts of ourselves that have been hurt. In this way, healing becomes an act of self-love and resilience, a testament to the strength that lies within us all.

As we navigate this path, we learn that healing is not just about mending what is broken, but also about growing stronger and more compassionate. It transforms our wounds into wisdom and our pain into purpose, allowing us to emerge from the darkness with renewed hope and a deeper understanding of ourselves and the world around us.

"Though He slay me, yet will I trust Him."

—Job 13:15

Trust doesn't ignore pain. It leans into God anyway.

It acknowledges the struggles and embraces faith, even when the path seems uncertain. Amid trials, trust becomes a powerful anchor, grounding us in hope and resilience. It teaches us to see beyond our current circumstances, to find strength in vulnerability, and to believe in a greater purpose unfolding. Trust invites us to walk courageously, knowing that we are guided by a wisdom that transcends our understanding. It reminds us that even in the darkest moments, there is a light that never fades, a promise that never breaks.

"Jesus wept."

—John 11:35

He doesn't just fix grief. He shares it.

In this powerful moment, we see the depth of empathy and compassion that defines His character. It serves as a poignant reminder that in our own moments of sorrow and loss, we are not alone. Grief is not something to be swiftly mended or dismissed; it is a profound human experience that deserves acknowledgment and understanding. By sharing in our tears, He demonstrates that vulnerability is not a weakness but a bridge that connects us to one another, fostering a sense of community and support. As we navigate the complexities of life, this shared experience can offer solace and strength, encouraging us to extend the same compassion to others in their times of need.

Prayer & Practice Prompt

Prayer

Father, I don't bring much today—just what hurts. I lay it before You, not wrapped in answers, but in hope. Let even this wound become worship. Let even this ache become an altar. Amen.

Practice

Set aside a quiet space this week. Don't rush to explain or fix what you're feeling. Just name it. Sit with God in it. And if you can, write a short prayer or journal entry—not to impress, but to release.

Pilgrim's Pause

Journaling Prompt:

What wound are you tempted to hide? What would it look like to bring it honestly into God's presence?

In the quiet sanctuary of my thoughts, I ponder the wounds I often tuck away from the world's prying eyes. These scars, invisible yet deeply etched in my spirit, whisper stories of past hurts and fears. Bringing them into God's presence feels like shedding layers of armor, revealing the tender vulnerability beneath.

It would be a moment of cathartic release, where honesty paves the path to healing. In that sacred space, the light of divine love would gently begin to mend the broken pieces, offering comfort and strength. Embracing this process requires courage and faith, knowing that in the act of unveiling, there lies the promise of renewal and hope.

Group Reflection:

How can our communities make space for honest, unpolished worship—the kind that bleeds before it heals?

How can we come together to create environments where authenticity is valued over perfection? One way is by fostering open dialogues that encourage sharing personal stories and experiences without judgment. We can build supportive networks where individuals feel safe to express their true selves, knowing they are surrounded by understanding and empathetic peers.

Another approach is to embrace diverse expressions of worship, recognizing that each person's journey is unique and worthy of respect. By celebrating differences, we can enrich our collective experience and deepen our connections with one another.

Additionally, providing platforms for creativity, such as art, music, and writing, can be powerful mediums for unpolished worship. These outlets allow individuals to express their emotions and struggles in raw, meaningful ways that resonate with others.

Ultimately, making space for honest worship involves compassion, openness, and a willingness to embrace vulnerability, fostering a sense of community that nurtures growth and healing for all involved.

8
The Ledge Where Trust Was Born

"Though He slay me, yet will I trust Him..."

"Standing on the Brink of Trust"

Charles E. Cravey

I found no path, no bridge, no sign—

Just air and echo, rock and sky.

Behind me, loss; ahead, no line—

Only the space where fears can fly.

I did not leap. I did not flee.

I stood where silence dares to break.

And in the hush, He said to me:

"This is the ground where trust will wake."

No guarantee, no map unfurled—

Just Presence whispering through the storm.

And there, between the edge and the world,

I found a faith both fierce and warm.

So, if you reach that bitter brink,

Do not despair, nor curse the height.

For trust is born not where we think—

But on the ledge, without the light.

Devotional Reflection: When the Edge Becomes the Altar

There's a kind of faith that forms in safety.

But the deepest trust—*the unshakable kind*—is often born on ledges. Those moments when all your planning, all your preparation, no longer hold weight. When the next step isn't visible.

Ledges feel like loss. But they often become the *birthing ground of revelation*.

"Trust in the Lord with all your heart, and lean not on your own understanding…" (Proverbs 3:5)

To trust is to loosen our grip on understanding. It's to believe—not blindly, but boldly—that the One who brought you this far will not vanish when the path does.

The ledge is not the end. It's where control is surrendered so that intimacy can begin.

In this surrender, we find a new kind of strength, one that is not dependent on our own abilities but grounded in faith. This act of trust opens doors to wisdom and peace, allowing us to navigate life's uncertainties with a sense of purpose and calm.

As we let go of the need to have all the answers, we create space for growth, healing, and the transformative power of divine guidance. Each step forward, though perhaps hesitant, is a testament to our courage and commitment to a journey that is much richer than we could ever map out alone.

"The eternal God is your dwelling place, and underneath are the everlasting arms..."

—Deuteronomy 33:27

You may not see the arms. But they are always there.

They cradle you in moments of doubt, offering solace when the world feels overwhelming. In times of joy, they lift you higher, celebrating your triumphs and enveloping you in warmth. These unseen arms are a constant presence, a source of strength and comfort that guides you through life's journey.

Trust in their quiet support. Just as the roots of a mighty tree remain hidden yet steadfast, these arms provide a foundation upon which you can always rely. Embrace the peace that comes from knowing you are never alone, held in love that is both timeless and boundless.

A Pilgrim's Glimpse: When I Had to Let Go

There was a time when I had to part with something I cherished deeply.

A ministry role that had profoundly shaped and stretched me, allowing me to invest in others. Yet, deep down, I sensed God urging me that the moment had come. The fruit had withered. My spirit was becoming weary. Yet, I held on tightly.

Until I could no longer do so.

The day I walked away, I found myself alone in my car, crying. Not out of doubt in God—but because I *had to place my trust in Him more than I wished to.*

That leap didn't immediately lead to something new. It was merely... stillness. A period of waiting.

But in that stillness, I discovered a lesson: faith that *waits* is just as strong as faith that *acts*. Sometimes, it may even be more powerful.

Eventually, new opportunities arose. Yet, even if they had not, God met me on that ledge. And that was more than enough.

Scripture Focus: Anchored in Midair

"Even though I walk through the valley of the shadow of death, I will fear no evil, for You are with me..."

—Psalm 23:4

He doesn't promise shortcuts—He promises presence.

Amid trials and tribulations, this assurance becomes a beacon of hope and strength. Life's journey may take us through dark and uncertain paths, yet the knowledge that we are not alone empowers us to face each challenge with courage and resilience. The promise of divine companionship offers solace and a sense of peace, reminding us that we are supported and loved, no matter the circumstances. Embracing this presence transforms our perspective, allowing us to see light even in the shadows and to find grace in the journey itself.

"The eternal God is your refuge, and underneath are the everlasting arms."

—Deuteronomy 33:27

The arms you can't see are still strong enough to hold you. They cradle you in moments of doubt and lift you in times of despair. These unseen arms are a source of unwavering support, carrying you through life's trials and tribulations with grace and resilience. Just as a gentle breeze can be felt but not seen, this divine presence offers comfort and strength, reminding you that you are never truly alone. In a world that often feels uncertain, the assurance of these everlasting arms provides a foundation of hope and peace, guiding you forward with love and light.

"He makes my feet like the feet of a deer; He enables me to tread on the heights."

—Habakkuk 3:19

Even on ledges, He gives us footing.

With each step, we find stability and strength, a sense of confidence that propels us forward. The path may be steep and the journey daunting, yet we are equipped with the grace and agility to navigate even the most challenging terrains.

This divine assurance allows us to embrace the heights, to rise above the valleys of doubt and fear, and to stand tall amidst the peaks of our endeavors. Each ledge becomes not a limitation but an opportunity to pause, reflect, and marvel at the progress we have made, knowing that we are guided and supported every step of the way.

Prayer & Practice Prompt

Prayer

Lord, the ledge frightens me. The unknown stretches wide and wild. But today, I choose to believe that You are not only ahead of me but beneath me. Teach me to trust when clarity is gone and let that trust carry me forward. Amen.

Practice

Stand somewhere elevated—a hill, a porch, or a ledge if it's safe—and take a few moments to breathe, pray, and reflect. Let the openness remind you that God meets us not just in boundaries, but in wide places of faith.

Pilgrim's Pause

Journaling Prompt:

Where in your life are you standing on the edge of uncertainty? What would trusting God look like there?

Taking a moment to reflect on the areas of life where uncertainty looms, one can often find themselves perched on the precipice of decisions and opportunities that feel daunting. Trusting God in these moments might look like surrendering the need for control and choosing to have faith in a greater plan. It involves embracing the unknown with the belief that there is a purpose to the journey, even if the path ahead is unclear.

This trust could manifest as a sense of peace amidst chaos or the courage to take a step forward when fear tries to hold you back. It may mean daily prayers or meditations, seeking guidance and strength to navigate the challenges.

Trusting God could also involve listening to your inner voice, tuning into the wisdom that speaks softly in your heart, and aligning your actions with love and compassion. As you lean into this trust, you might discover a newfound resilience and a deeper sense of connection to the world around you, knowing that you are supported in ways you cannot yet see.

Group Reflection:

Have you ever stood on a life "ledge"—between endings and beginnings? What sustained you in that space?

In those moments teetering on the edge between what was and what will be, it's often hope and resilience that provide the most steadfast support. This in-between space, though daunting, can be a powerful place for transformation. Many find solace in reflecting on past experiences, drawing strength from lessons learned and the knowledge that they have navigated uncertainties before.

Community and connection also play crucial roles in sustaining us. Reaching out to friends, family, or mentors can offer comfort and perspective, reminding us that we are not alone in our journey. Engaging in creative activities, whether it be writing, painting, or music, can also provide an outlet for expression and a way to process emotions.

Moreover, mindfulness practices, such as meditation or yoga, can help ground us in the present, fostering a sense of calm amidst the chaos. Embracing the unknown with curiosity rather than fear can transform this precarious ledge into a launchpad for growth and new beginnings. Each step forward, however small, becomes a testament to our courage and capacity for renewal.

9
The Silence Between the Psalms

"Be still, and know..."

"The Rest Between the Notes"

Charles E. Cravey

I sang when joy was fresh and wide,

And cried when grief held tight its chord—

But now I sit where both have died,

And wait without a single word.

The melody has ceased to rise.

The echoes fade, the stanza still —

Yet even here, beneath closed skies,

A deeper tune begins to fill.

It doesn't shout or strike a chord—

It hums beneath the breath of prayer.

A holy hush the heart affords

When words dissolve in sacred air.

So let me sit in Psalm-less grace,

And trust that silence isn't lack—

For even now, in stillest place,

His unseen music calls me back.

Devotional Reflection: The Sacred Sound of Stillness

Between David's praises and his laments lies *silence*.

Moments where no psalm is penned, no prayer recorded. Yet we know he lived them—those long stretches where the heart feels blank. Not rebellious. Not faithless. Just... waiting.

In our walk, we often rush to fill the silence. But what if the pause is part of the music?

"Be still, and know that I am God..." (Psalm 46:10)

Stillness isn't inactivity—it's holy attention.

It is a profound pause in the midst of life's chaos, an opportunity to attune oneself to the divine presence that often goes unnoticed in the hustle and bustle of daily routines. In this sacred quietude, clarity emerges, and the noise of the world fades away, allowing the heart to hear the whispers of wisdom and peace.

This sacred stillness invites introspection and reflection, encouraging us to connect with our innermost selves and the spiritual truths that guide us. It's a reminder that in the silence, there is strength, and in the pause, there is purpose. By embracing this holy attention, we open ourselves to a deeper understanding of our place in the universe and the gentle guidance of a higher power.

Amid stillness, we discover a sanctuary for the soul—a space where we can surrender our worries and fears, trusting that we are held in the embrace of something greater. It is in this tranquil state that we find renewal, inspiration, and the courage to move forward with grace and love.

The silence between the psalms is where the Spirit reminds us that our worth is not in constant outpouring, but in *presence*. That God is not merely the recipient of our songs but the composer of the rests between them.

It's not a void. It's a verse being written slowly.

"For God alone my soul waits in silence..." (Psalm 62:1)

A profound peace envelops me as I find solace in the quiet moments of reflection. In these times, the noise of the world fades away, and I am reminded of the strength and comfort that faith brings. It is in this sacred stillness that I can connect deeply with my inner self and the divine presence, finding guidance and hope for the journey ahead. As I trust and surrender, I am reassured that I am never alone and that patience and faith will illuminate my path.

A Pilgrim's Glimpse: The Week My Words Left Me

There was a week—longer, really—when I found I couldn't pray.

The words just… slipped away. I sat in the morning with my Bible open, journal in hand, coffee warm beside me—and nothing. No tears. No revelations. Just blank space.

At first, it troubled me. I thought something was wrong. But slowly, I sensed that God wasn't disappointed. He was *present*. Not demanding a speech—just inviting a silence.

So I kept showing up.

Not with eloquence, but with availability.

And in time, the silence softened. Peace grew, not from what I said, but from simply being with Him.

I still write and speak and pray aloud. But I'll never forget the holy hush of that week—where I learned God's favorite room might just be the quiet one.

Scripture Focus: Stillness That Speaks

"Be still before the Lord and wait patiently for Him..."

—**Psalm 37:7**

Stillness is not delay. It is devotion in pause.

It is a moment of reflection, allowing oneself to be open to the whispers of wisdom and guidance. In this sacred pause, the clamor of the world fades, and the heart finds solace in quietude. Patience becomes a gentle companion, teaching us the art of trust and surrender. As we embrace this stillness, we create space for grace to unfold and for divine clarity to illuminate our path. Here, in the tranquility of waiting, we discover strength, purpose, and the profound beauty of faith.

"The Lord is in His holy temple; let all the earth keep silence before Him."

—**Habakkuk 2:20**

Sometimes reverence means *quiet*.

It is in the quiet moments that we find the profound ability to reflect and connect with the divine. Silence offers a space where the noise of the world fades away, allowing us to listen deeply to the inner whispers of our hearts. In these peaceful pauses, we can discover a sense of awe and wonder, a reminder of the greater mysteries that surround us.

Through this stillness, we honor the sacred presence that dwells within and around us, a presence that often speaks not in thunderous declarations but in the gentle rustle of leaves and the soft glow of a sunset. Let us cherish these moments of quietude, for they hold the power to illuminate our path and bring us closer to the essence of reverence itself.

"...a time to keep silent, and a time to speak."

—Ecclesiastes 3:7

Even wisdom knows when not to say a word.

In the delicate dance of life, silence can be more powerful than words. It is in the quiet moments that we often find clarity, contemplation, and the space to listen—not just to others, but to our own inner voices. The art of knowing when to speak and when to remain silent is a skill honed by those who understand the nuances of communication and the impact of their words.

When we choose silence, we allow ourselves the opportunity to observe and absorb the world around us, to learn from it, and to respond with intention and empathy. It is in these pauses that we can connect more deeply with others, showing respect and understanding that words alone sometimes fail to convey.

Conversely, when the time comes to speak, let our words be chosen with care and purpose, carrying the weight of our thoughts and the sincerity of our hearts. Whether in moments of joy or sorrow, in times of conflict or peace, may our voices rise to uplift, to heal, and to inspire, leaving echoes of kindness and wisdom in their wake.

Prayer & Practice Prompt

Prayer

Lord, I confess—I fill the silence because it scares me. I think if You're quiet, You must be distant. But let me learn to sit with You in the hush. Let me trust that You are *still speaking*, even when You say nothing at all. Amen.

Practice

Spend five minutes in absolute quiet with God today. No requests. No Scripture. Just presence. Let the silence speak—and write down anything you feel or sense afterward.

Pilgrim's Pause

Journaling Prompt:

How do you respond when God feels quiet? What fears or peace rise up in you when the silence lingers?

In those moments when God feels quiet, I find myself turning inward, seeking solace in the stillness. Initially, a wave of uncertainty may wash over me, as if I'm navigating through uncharted waters without a compass. Questions swirl in my mind, tinged with the fear of being forgotten or unheard. Yet, as I sit with this silence, something profound begins to unfold.

I start to notice the subtle beauty that surrounds me—the rustling of leaves in the gentle breeze, the soft glow of the morning light filtering through my window. It is in this space of quietude that I discover a deeper sense of peace, a reminder that even in silence, there is presence.

I am encouraged to trust in the unseen, to have faith in the unfolding of a greater plan.

This period of stillness becomes an invitation to reflect, to listen more intently to the whispers of my own heart. It is a time to cultivate patience and to embrace the mystery, knowing that growth often occurs in the moments between the noise and the answers. In the end, the silence is not an absence but a profound opportunity to connect with the divine in an intimate and transformative way.

Group Reflection:

In what ways can we practice and honor spiritual stillness together—not just in music, but in shared life?

Gathering in communal silence, through meditation or prayer, can create a powerful shared experience of spiritual stillness. Setting aside time for group reflection, where each person can share their thoughts and feelings without judgment, fosters deep connection and understanding. Engaging in mindful activities, such as nature walks or art creation, allows everyone to slow down and appreciate the present moment together. Practicing gratitude as a group, by sharing what we are thankful for, can also cultivate a sense of peace and contentment. By creating spaces where open-hearted listening and support are prioritized, we can honor and nurture the spiritual stillness that resides within each of us, strengthening our bonds and enriching our shared journey.

10
The Cup That Didn't Pass

"Yet not My will, but Yours be done…"

"The Garden Where He Stayed"

Charles E. Cravey

I knelt where olives bend and groan,

Where silence drips from midnight leaves.

He prayed a prayer He'd die alone—

And found no hand that stays or grieves.

The cup did not slide from His grip.

Though trembling lips had begged it gone.

He tasted sorrow's final sip—

And stayed until the dawn had drawn.

No sword was drawn to hold back pain.

No voice from Heaven split the air.

He bore the crush, the weight, the strain—

A lamb where lions didn't dare.

So here I kneel in lesser night,

And find my tears in kindred dust.

I drink the ache and choose the light—

For He has shown that grief can trust.

Devotional Reflection: The Prayer That Wasn't Answered—Yet Was

In Gethsemane, Jesus didn't whisper platitudes.

He groaned. He bled. He asked for escape. "Father, if it be possible, let this cup pass from Me…"

And still—the cup did not pass.

What are we to make of that?

That even the Son of God was not spared the furnace of obedience? That pain was not avoided but *redeemed*?

Gethsemane teaches us this: **even unanswered prayers can glorify God.** Not because they fail—but because surrender speaks louder than escape.

"He learned obedience through what He suffered..." (Hebrews 5:8)

Jesus didn't need to be purified—but He did *enter fully into our humanity* by walking the road we fear most: the one we cannot avoid.

Your Gethsemane may not come with thorns or whips, but it will come. A moment when the soul must choose faith—not in spite of sorrow, but through it.

And when it does, know this: Jesus has *already been there*. The garden is not empty.

A Pilgrim's Glimpse: My Own Gethsemane

There was a year—heavy and gray—when everything I loved seemed to crumble at once.

A family fracture. A ministry unraveling. Health issues that came without warning or remedy. I remember praying in the dark, fists clenched, tears hot: "God, take it. Change it. Fix it."

He didn't. Not right away. Not in the way I imagined.

But He stayed.

I didn't get the miracle I asked for. But I received something else—*companionship*. In the ache. In the slow days. In the hollow of that cup.

Over time, I came to realize something strange: that year became the doorway to deeper compassion, steadier joy, and a love that didn't hinge on circumstances.

The cup didn't pass. But neither did *He*.

Scripture Focus: The Weight of the Will

"My soul is overwhelmed with sorrow to the point of death… yet not My will, but Yours be done."

—Matthew 26:38–39

True surrender is not the absence of emotion, but obedience through anguish.

It is the act of trusting in a greater plan, even when the path seems shrouded in darkness. In moments of deep despair, when the weight of the world feels unbearable, surrender becomes a beacon of hope. It is the quiet courage to let go of control and embrace the unknown with faith.

In the garden of Gethsemane, Jesus exemplified this profound surrender. His heart was heavy with the knowledge of the suffering that lay ahead, yet His resolve remained unshaken. This powerful testament to obedience and faith serves as an inspiration to those who face their own trials.

True surrender invites us to lean into our vulnerabilities and to find strength in the divine promise that we are never alone. It reminds us that through our struggles, we can discover resilience and grace, emerging stronger and more compassionate. As we navigate life's challenges, may we find solace in the knowledge that surrender is not a sign of weakness but a testament to the enduring power of faith.

"He offered up prayers and petitions... with loud cries and tears..."

—Hebrews 5:7

Even Jesus cried aloud in prayer. Let yours be raw and unfiltered, a true reflection of your heart's deepest desires and struggles. In moments of vulnerability, when words may fail, let your tears speak the language of your soul. Embrace the authenticity of your emotions, knowing that every heartfelt plea is heard and cherished. Whether in solitude or amidst the support of loved ones, allow yourself the grace to express your innermost thoughts and fears. For in these honest moments, we find connection and comfort and the strength to face whatever challenges lie ahead.

"For the joy set before Him, He endured the cross…"

—Hebrews 12:2

The cup was bitter. But joy stood beyond it. The path was fraught with trials and tribulations, yet the promise of redemption and the hope of a brighter tomorrow lent strength to weary souls. Each step taken was underpinned by an unwavering faith and an unyielding belief in the power of love and sacrifice. It was this profound understanding that transformed suffering into a conduit for grace and salvation.

In the end, it was not the burden of the cross that defined the journey, but the boundless joy and eternal peace that awaited on the other side. This journey, marked by courage and perseverance, offered a profound testament to the resilience of the human spirit and the transformative power of unwavering hope.

Prayer & Practice Prompt

Prayer

Father, I do not ask for suffering—but if it must come, let it come with You. Teach me what it means to hold the cup and still say "yes." Let my fear become faith, and my struggle become surrender. Amen.

Practice

Write a letter to God you never plan to send. Pour out the prayer you're afraid to pray aloud. Be unfiltered. Gethsemane wasn't quiet—it was honest. Let this be your garden of truth.

Pilgrim's Pause

Journaling Prompt:

What "cup" have you asked to pass? How have you seen God remain—even when the answer was "not yet" or "no"?

When faced with life's challenges, there are moments when we wish certain burdens could be lifted from our shoulders. One such "cup" I asked to pass was the overwhelming pressure of a demanding job that consumed every waking moment. Yet, despite my pleas for a change, the situation remained unchanged for quite some time.

In those moments of uncertainty, I found comfort in recognizing the subtle ways God remained present. Through supportive colleagues who offered encouragement, unexpected opportunities for growth, and quiet moments of reflection that provided clarity, I realized that while the answer was "not yet," it did not mean I was alone.

This experience taught me valuable lessons in patience and resilience, and I discovered strength I didn't know I possessed. In hindsight, the journey through those challenging times equipped me with skills and insights that prepared me for future endeavors. It was a gentle reminder that even when life doesn't unfold as planned, there is a greater tapestry being woven, and each thread has its purpose.

Group Reflection:

How do we walk with others through their Gethsemanes—not with quick advice, but with presence?

By offering a listening ear and an open heart, we can truly be there for others. It's about creating a safe space where they feel comfortable expressing their fears and feelings. We can show empathy and understanding, acknowledging their struggles without judgment. Sometimes, the most profound support comes from simply being there, sharing the silence, and offering a comforting presence that assures them they are not alone.

Furthermore, small gestures of kindness, such as a gentle touch or a warm smile, can speak volumes, providing solace and strength in their time of need.

11

The Table in the Wilderness

"You prepare a table before me..."

Bread in Barren Places

Charles E. Cravey

I wandered through a silent land.

Where thorns grew thick and hope grew thin.

But there He met me—outstretched hand—

And laid a feast I'd missed within.

No palace shone, no choirs sang,

Just desert dust and cypress lean.

Yet still the scent of heaven rang.

Where grace had touched the in-between.

My cup ran over, scarred, and full.

My soul was fed while shadows stayed.

The barren broke, the winds grew still —

When hunger knelt where mercy lay.

So now I seek not only light

But Him who breaks the bread in the dark.

His wilderness becomes delight.

When love has kindled famine's spark.

Devotional Reflection: Presence, Not Escape

God prepares tables in strange places.

We expect celebration after the trial. He serves it *during*. He lays the linen in wilderness seasons—when enemies lurk and hope is still fragile.

"You prepare a table before me in the presence of my enemies..." (Psalm 23:5)

This is not just provision—it's communion. Not just nourishment—but nearness.

In Exodus, God gave manna *daily*, not because He couldn't provide more—but because He *wanted to teach dependence*. The desert wasn't just a detour. It was a dining room.

How often we pray to escape the desert, while God invites us to *dine in it*.

"The Lord your God... humbled you and tested you... feeding you with manna to teach you that man does not live by bread alone..." (Deut. 8:3)

The table in the wilderness teaches us this: *His presence is the meal.*

A Pilgrim's Glimpse: The Night I Tasted Peace in a Hospital Room

I remember sitting in a quiet hospital room beside someone I love. Machines hummed, fluorescent lights buzzed low, and the night felt heavy.

There were no answers. Just questions. Fear hovered like mist.

And yet—there, in that wilderness—I felt something almost contradictory: peace. Not because things were okay, but because *God was so present* I could almost feel the weight of His robe in the room.

That night, I didn't ask for signs. I didn't have grand prayers.

I just sat. Wept a little. Whispered thanks. And somehow—I was full.

That's the table. That's the feast. A love that comes not after the valley, *but within it.*

Scripture Focus: The Feast in the Barren Field

"You prepare a table before me in the presence of my enemies..."

—Psalm 23:5

Joy doesn't wait for the enemy to leave. It rises while they watch. It shines brightly, unfazed by the shadows that linger nearby. Amid adversity, joy becomes a beacon, illuminating the path forward with courage and resilience. It whispers to the soul, reminding us that even in the face of trials, there is a strength within that cannot be diminished. This joy is not passive; it is a powerful force that transforms fear into hope and despair into determination.

As we embrace this joy, we find ourselves empowered to rise above challenges, to dance in defiance of doubt, and to celebrate life in all its vibrant complexity. It is a reminder that our spirit is unbreakable and that even in the darkest moments, light can burst forth, bringing warmth and inspiration to all who witness it.

"They will neither hunger nor thirst... for He who has compassion on them will guide them and lead them beside springs of water."

—Isaiah 49:10

Provision is never far from the compassionate hand.

It is a reminder that even in the most challenging times, there is a source of comfort and sustenance waiting to be discovered. This promise resonates through the ages, offering hope to those who seek solace. The journey may be arduous, but with faith and trust, every step is guided by a compassionate force that ensures our needs are met.

In our daily lives, this can be seen in the unexpected kindness of strangers, the support of loved ones, and the resilience we find within ourselves. It encourages us to extend the same compassion to others, creating a ripple effect of care and understanding. As we walk through life, let us remember to seek out these springs of water—not just for our own refreshment, but to share with those who wander in search of their own oasis.

"Jesus took bread, gave thanks, and broke it…"

—Luke 22:19

He still breaks bread—especially when the world breaks us.

In moments of despair and heartache, when it feels like the weight of the world is too much to bear, the simple act of breaking bread becomes a profound symbol of hope and renewal. It is a reminder that even in times of brokenness, there is an opportunity for healing and connection. Sharing a meal can bring people together, fostering a sense of community and belonging.

Just as bread is broken to be shared, our own experiences of hardship can become sources of strength and compassion for others. By reaching out and supporting one another, we create a tapestry of resilience and love. Through these connections, we find the courage to rebuild and the grace to move forward, knowing that we are never truly alone.

Prayer & Practice Prompt

Prayer

Lord, I confess—I want deliverance more than dwelling. But teach me to sit at Your table, even in the wild places. Help me taste joy that doesn't depend on outcome and to find You where fear once stood. Amen.

Practice

Set a simple table this week—just for a meal or even a cup of tea. Light a candle. Sit in silence with God. Let this become your wilderness table, your invitation to presence. Write down what you feel or hear in the quiet.

Pilgrim's Pause

Journaling Prompt:

Where have you experienced unexpected grace in a barren place? What did that table look like—and how did it feed your soul?

The memory of that moment remains vivid, like a treasured photograph tucked away in my heart. It was during a solo camping trip in the vast Appalachian Mountains. The landscape stretched endlessly, a sea of trees and stones under an unyielding sun. I had begun the journey seeking solitude, hoping the quiet would offer me clarity.

Unexpectedly, amidst the desolation, I stumbled upon a small oasis. It was a humble patch of greenery, a marvelous contrast to the surrounding woods. The table, in this metaphorical sense, was nature's own altar—a flat stone shaded by a lone, stubborn hickory tree. I sat there, feeling the soft whisper of the breeze and listening to the gentle rustle of leaves.

This unexpected grace was a feast for my soul. The simplicity of the scene nourished me, reminding me of life's resilience and beauty. It was as if the universe had laid out a banquet, not of food, but of peace and reflection. In that serene silence, I found a deeper connection to myself, a renewed appreciation for the quiet strength that lies within every heart.

Group Reflection:

How can we become "table-bearers" for others in their wilderness? What does it look like to prepare a table for someone else's struggle?

To become "table-bearers" for others in their wilderness means to offer support, comfort, and sustenance during their challenging times. It involves being present, listening without judgment, and providing a safe space for them to express their fears and hopes. This act of kindness can manifest in many ways:

1. **Empathy and Understanding**: Truly listen to their stories and experiences without interrupting or offering immediate solutions. Sometimes, just knowing someone is there to listen can be incredibly comforting.

2. **Practical Support**: Offer tangible help, whether it's cooking a meal, running errands, or helping with responsibilities that may be overwhelming during a difficult period.

3. **Emotional Encouragement**: Send encouraging messages or reminders that they are not alone and that their feelings are valid. A simple note or call can uplift their spirits.

4. **Creating Safe Spaces**: Invite them to a physical or metaphorical table where they feel safe to share their burdens. This could be a coffee shop chat or a walk in the park where they can unwind.

5. **Patience and Presence**: Sometimes, just being there in silence is enough. Your presence can be a comforting reminder

that they are supported.

Preparing a table for someone else's struggle is about being a steady, reliable presence in their life, offering them the grace and space to heal and grow in their own time. This generosity of spirit not only aids them but also enriches our own lives with deeper connections and understanding.

12

Thorns in the Path

"There was given me a thorn..."

The Thorn and the Trail

Charles E. Cravey

I prayed for smoothness in the road.

For flowers soft beneath my tread.

But thorns arose where comfort slowed,

And every bruised petal had bled.

I cursed the sting, then heard it speak—

Not as a foe, but sacred flare.

"This pain," it said, "will make you weak,

So, grace may hold you stronger there."

The path grew tight, the branches tore,

Yet in the scrape, I came to see

The One who wore a crown of thorns

Still walks the wounded way with me.

So let the trail be laced with pain—

I do not walk it now alone.

The thorn may pierce, but not in vain—

For mercy marks where blood has flown.

Devotional Reflection: Wounded Yet Walking

Paul's "thorn in the flesh" was never named. Scholars guess it could have been physical, emotional, or spiritual. But God left it unnamed so *all of us* could find ourselves in it.

"Three times I pleaded… But He said to me, 'My grace is sufficient for you…'" (2 Corinthians 12:8–9)

Some wounds won't heal the way we want. Some struggles remain, not because God is cruel—but because His grace becomes visible *through* them.

The thorn humbles. It slows us. It keeps us leaning.

"For when I am weak, then I am strong."

This is not resignation—it's recognition. The thorn is not the enemy. Pride is. And weakness is not the failure. Hiding is.

So, we walk, not despite the thorn—but with it. And in doing so, discover that our limp becomes our testimony.

A Pilgrim's Glimpse: A Limp That Led Me Deeper

There was a stretch of time when I wrestled with anxiety. Not situational nerves, but chronic, unwelcome fear—whispers of dread at the edge of everything.

I prayed. Fought. Begged.

And it didn't vanish.

I expected deliverance. What I got was *companionship*. A growing capacity to weep with others. To pause longer in prayer. To teach not from perfection but from presence.

I still feel it sometimes. But it no longer defines me. And strangely, I thank God for what it opened in me—a softer voice, a slower pace, and a gospel not coated in plastic.

The thorn didn't win. But it did witness.

Scripture Focus: Grace in the Bruise

"My grace is sufficient for you, for My power is made perfect in weakness."

—2 Corinthians 12:9

Weakness is not a barrier—it's a channel. It allows us to connect more deeply with ourselves and others, fostering empathy and understanding. When we embrace our vulnerabilities, we open ourselves to growth and transformation. In recognizing our limitations, we make space for divine strength to manifest in our lives, guiding us through challenges and illuminating paths we might never have discovered on our own.

In a world that often celebrates invulnerability, acknowledging our weaknesses can feel counterintuitive. Yet, it is in these moments of humility that we truly learn the value of resilience and the beauty of surrendering control. By accepting our imperfections, we invite grace to work within us, transforming our perceived shortcomings into powerful testimonies of faith and perseverance.

Through this journey, we come to understand that true strength lies not in the absence of weakness, but in the courage to face it head-on, trusting that we are supported by a greater force that loves us unconditionally.

"Surely He has borne our griefs and carried our sorrows..."

—Isaiah 53:4

He carried thorns before we did.

He wore a crown of sacrifice, woven with the pain and redemption of humanity. In every step He took, He bore the weight of our burdens, transforming suffering into a testament of love and resilience. His journey was a path of empathy and compassion, reminding us that we are never alone in our struggles. Through His actions, He taught us the power of grace, and the strength found in selfless service to others. As we reflect on His enduring legacy, we find hope and inspiration to carry our own burdens with dignity and faith.

"He was given a crown of thorns and mocked..."

—Mark 15:17

Every thorn we wear, He wore first.

In His suffering, we find a reflection of our own struggles and pain. Yet, in this shared experience, there is also a profound sense of hope and redemption. The crown of thorns, a symbol of scorn and suffering, becomes a testament to resilience and grace. It reminds us that even in the depths of adversity, there is the possibility of rising above, of transforming pain into strength and compassion.

As we navigate life's challenges, we can draw inspiration from this powerful image. It encourages us to face our trials with courage and to extend empathy to others who are burdened by their own "crowns." In doing so, we honor the legacy of enduring love and unwavering faith, finding solace in the knowledge that we are never alone in our journey.

Prayer & Practice Prompt

Prayer

Lord, I bring my thorn—not with bitterness, but with honesty. I wanted You to take it. But if You choose to leave it, leave it with grace. Let this wound become a window, and my struggle a sanctuary. Amen.

Practice

Name your thorn—privately or aloud. Then write down what it's taught you. Don't sanitize it—be real. Keep it somewhere visible this week, not as shame, but as strength revealed through weakness.

Pilgrim's Pause

Journaling Prompt:

What "thorn" have you carried—and how has God met you there?

This reflective question invites you to delve deep into a personal challenge or struggle, symbolized by the "thorn," that you've faced. Think about a difficulty that has been a persistent part of your life—something that may have caused pain or discomfort yet also led to growth or insight.

As you ponder this, consider how your faith or spirituality has played a role in addressing this challenge. How has God, or your understanding of a higher power, provided comfort, guidance, or strength through this journey? You've found solace in prayer, support from a community, or moments of unexpected grace that helped you persevere.

In writing about your experiences, allow yourself to explore the emotions and lessons that arose from carrying this thorn. Reflect on how this challenge has shaped who you are today and the ways in which your faith has been a source of resilience and hope.

Group Reflection:

How do we talk about weakness in Christian community? What would it look like to honor the thorn, not just the victory?

In Christian community, discussing weakness can be a profound act of vulnerability and strength. It invites members to embrace their humanity and recognize that imperfection is a shared experience. Rather than viewing weakness as something to be hidden, it can be seen as an opportunity for growth and connection.

Honoring the thorn alongside the victory means acknowledging that struggles are an integral part of one's faith journey. It involves creating a space where individuals feel safe to share their burdens without fear of judgment. By doing so, the community can support each other in their challenges, offering compassion and understanding.

This approach can be enriched by stories and teachings from scripture that highlight how moments of weakness often lead to deeper faith and reliance on divine strength. For example, the Apostle Paul spoke of a "thorn in the flesh" that kept him humble and reliant on God's grace. In this way, the thorn becomes a symbol of how divine power is made perfect in human frailty.

By honoring both the thorns and the victories, a Christian community can foster an environment of authenticity and mutual support, where every member feels valued and uplifted, regardless of their struggles. This balance encourages a holistic approach to spiritual life, reminding everyone that strength is often found in acknowledging and embracing one's weaknesses.

13
The Watchman's Light

"I wait for the Lord, more than watchmen wait for the morning..."

"The Flame That Would Not Sleep"

Charles E. Cravey

I stood upon the midnight wall,

Where silence stretched and stars withdrew.

I saw no sign, no clarion call—

Just shadow's weight and aching blue.

But still I held the lantern high,

Though wind and doubt pressed hard and wide.

For in the black, one cannot lie—

A single flame defies the tide.

I did not know how long to stay.

Nor when the light would break the gray.

I only knew this post was mine—

To stand, to hope, to mark the day.

And when the dawn began to breathe,

It kissed the oil upon my skin.

The watchman's task was not beneath—

It lit the world by waiting in.

Devotional Reflection: Hope That Keeps Watch

Waiting can feel like failure.

To be still, to endure, to remain—these aren't celebrated in a culture obsessed with immediacy. But Scripture teaches that *waiting is not weakness—it is spiritual strength wearing stillness as armor.*

"I wait for the Lord... and in His word I put my hope..." (Psalm 130:5)

The watchman isn't idle. He is **anchored**. He watches not because he doubts the morning, but because he "believes it is coming."

Some seasons don't demand motion—they demand **persistence**. And the flicker of a heart still turned toward Heaven is a greater act of praise than most notice.

"Those who wait for the Lord will renew their strength..." (Isaiah 40:31)

We don't just wait for the light. We **become** it.

A Pilgrim's Glimpse: The Letter I Kept Writing

I once wrote a letter I never sent.

It was a prayer in the shape of a note—addressed to God, to someone I loved, or maybe to myself. I wrote it during a time when doors seemed welded shut and answers came only in echoes.

I tucked it in my Bible.

Every few weeks, I'd read it again. Sometimes I wept. Sometimes I wondered if I should toss it. But something made me keep it—not out of denial, but *devotion*.

Months passed. Change came, quietly. Peace returned in pieces. And I realized one day—my prayer hadn't gone unanswered. It had gone **underground**. And God had been nourishing it in the dark.

The letter still rests between the pages. But now, it feels less like longing and more like light.

Scripture Focus: Vigilance and Victory

"More than watchmen wait for the morning..."

—**Psalm 130:6**

Real hope waits *with intention*—not passively but holding the lamp. The light within the lamp is a beacon, a promise of warmth and guidance through the darkest of nights. Real hope is an active force, a steadfast companion that fuels our spirits and keeps our eyes fixed on the horizon. It is the quiet strength that whispers, "Keep going," when the journey feels long and the path uncertain.

As the stars twinkle softly above, hope is the flame that refuses to falter, illuminating each step forward and casting away the shadows of doubt. It is the gentle reminder that even in the stillness, there is movement—an unseen choreography of dreams aligning with destiny.

In moments of waiting, we find the space to reflect, to nurture our inner light, and to prepare our hearts for the dawn. Because hope is not just about the arrival of morning; it's about embracing the journey through the night with courage and grace, knowing that every dawn brings new beginnings and endless possibilities.

"Though it linger, wait for it; it will certainly come…"

—Habakkuk 2:3

Delay is not denial. The dawn is timed to grace. The night may seem long and the shadows deep, but every moment of waiting is a seed planted in the fertile soil of patience. With each passing day, we are given opportunities to grow stronger and more resilient, learning to trust the timing of life's unfolding.

In the quiet moments of anticipation, we find room for reflection and gratitude, discovering the beauty in the pause. It's in this space that dreams are nurtured, taking root and preparing to bloom in their perfect season.

Remember, every sunrise brings new hope, each ray of light a gentle reminder that what is meant for us will find its way, illuminating our path with promises fulfilled. The journey may be slow, but every step taken is a testament to faith, courage, and the unyielding belief that all good things come in their own time.

"Let us not grow weary in doing good, for at the proper time we will reap a harvest..."

—Galatians 6:9

Watchmen don't stop sowing, even at night. They continue to plant seeds of hope and kindness, knowing that their efforts will one day blossom into something beautiful. In the quiet solitude of the night, they find strength and perseverance, guided by the stars and the gentle whispers of the wind. Their hearts are filled with unwavering faith, trusting that each small act contributes to a greater purpose.

As the moon casts its silver glow over the fields, the watchmen reflect on the cycles of life and the importance of nurturing what has been sown. They understand that patience and dedication are as crucial as the seeds themselves. In the darkness, they are reminded of the light that will eventually come, illuminating their path and bringing forth the fruits of their labor.

Through their tireless vigilance, they set an example for others, inspiring a community bound by shared dreams and aspirations. Together, they work towards a future where goodness flourishes, knowing that every effort, no matter how small, helps cultivate a world filled with compassion and understanding.

Prayer & Practice Prompt

Prayer

Lord, I am the watchman with tired arms. But I still lift the flame. Not because I see the light, but because I trust You are it. Renew my strength in the dark and let me welcome the morning when it comes. Amen.

Practice

Light a candle in your home one night this week. Sit with it for ten minutes—just breathing, praying, watching. Let it become your act of expectancy. The watchman's light is not loud, but it ***lingers***.

Pilgrim's Pause

Journaling Prompt:

What are you still waiting for? How has the waiting shaped you—and what light are you holding high?

As I ponder this question, I realize that I am still waiting for a sense of complete belonging, both within myself and in the world around me. This anticipation has taught me patience and resilience, molding me into someone who appreciates the beauty of the journey, not just the destination. It has opened my eyes to the subtleties of growth and the nuances of self-discovery.

The waiting has also kindled a light within me—a light of hope and optimism. I carry this light high, illuminating the path not only for myself but for others who may feel lost or in the dark. It is a beacon of encouragement, reminding me that while waiting can be challenging, it is also a time of preparation and transformation. This light fuels my passions and drives me to share kindness, understanding, and empathy with those I encounter. It is a reminder that every step, no matter how small, is a valuable part of the journey.

Group Reflection:

How can we be watchmen for each other—those who stand beside, hold the light, and whisper hope in the night?

To be watchmen for each other, we must cultivate a culture of empathy and understanding. It begins with active listening, where we truly hear and value each other's stories and struggles. By offering a shoulder to lean on and words of encouragement, we can help illuminate the path forward.

Creating a supportive environment means being present and available, checking in regularly, and offering assistance without judgment. We should celebrate each other's successes and provide comfort during challenging times. Sharing resources, whether they be time, knowledge, or even a simple gesture of kindness, can make a world of difference.

Moreover, fostering open communication builds trust, allowing us to speak up when we notice someone faltering. It's about being proactive rather than reactive, anticipating needs, and extending a hand before being asked.

Together, as a community of watchmen, we can weave a safety net of hope and resilience, ensuring that no one feels alone in their journey. Through collective strength and compassion, we can stand as beacons in the night, guiding each other toward brighter days.

14
Pilgrim's Benediction

"You have persevered and have endured hardships for My name..."

"The Road That Remains"

Charles E. Cravey

The dust still clings, the staff still worn,

The echoes of the road behind—

Yet even now, though bent and torn,

There burns a hope the dark can't bind.

I've tasted fog, I've known the flame,

I've walked where silence carved its creed.

But mercy met me, name by name,

And grace endured where I had need.

The gate was open, not because

I scaled with strength or climbed with pride—

But Love had lingered in my flaws.

And marked the miles I tried to hide.

So, if you walk where thorns still grow,

Or rest where river song is dim —

Take heart, O soul. The road you know

Has always led you back to Him.

Devotional Reflection: The Road Was Holy All Along

The journey is never just about arrival.

It's the footsteps, the falls, the moments of laughter and doubt, and the long in-betweens. The fog. The fire. The silence. The table. All of it.

"You have persevered… and have not grown weary." (Revelation 2:3)

Maybe not perfectly. Maybe not loudly. But *faithfully*.

We began this pilgrimage with trembling hands. And we end it with open ones—hands that held, released, and reached. Hands now marked by the sacred dust of the road.

The benediction is not *the end*. It's the blessing that says, "Go again. Rest as needed. But never forget—every stone you've stepped upon was known and woven into the map of God."

And now, having walked with the One who never left your side, you can offer what this world so desperately needs: a soul that's been to the edge… and chosen hope.

A Pilgrim's Glimpse: One Final Mile

There's a hill near my home that overlooks the fields—a small crest, nothing grand. I often walk there at dusk. One evening, after a long day of doubts and second-guessing, I paused there, looked out, and prayed quietly:

"Have I gone far enough? Have I said what I was meant to say?"

And I felt no booming voice. Just the softest assurance, gentle as wind through pine:

"You walked it. I was there."

That was enough.

If all I do is keep walking with Him and for Him—through pain, through poems, through daily yeses—then the pilgrimage will always be worth it.

And so will yours.

Scripture Focus: To the Faithful Road-Walker

"Well done, good and faithful servant... Enter into the joy of your Lord."

—Matthew 25:21

He doesn't measure by miles—but by motive.

He sees beyond the surface, peering into the depths of our hearts where true intentions reside. Every action, no matter how grand or humble, is weighed by the sincerity and love with which it is carried out. In this world, where achievements are often quantified by tangible successes, it is easy to overlook the quiet acts of kindness and the silent sacrifices made in the name of love or duty.

Yet, it is these very deeds, born from pure motives, that resonate in eternity and are cherished by the divine. Like a gardener tending to a hidden garden, nurturing each seed with care, the impact of our actions unfolds in ways we may never fully comprehend. Each gesture, fueled by genuine intent, plants seeds of hope and compassion, creating ripples that touch lives far beyond our immediate reach.

In this way, life invites us to focus not on the accolades or the applause, but on the integrity of our journey. And in doing so, we find that true joy emerges not from the destination, but from the path itself—the path that is illuminated by the light of our purest intentions.

"Let us hold unswervingly to the hope we profess, for He who promised is faithful."

—Hebrews 10:23

The road twists—but the Promise holds.

Through valleys of doubt and peaks of triumph, it remains steadfast, a guiding light in the darkest of times. Life's path may be fraught with unexpected turns and challenges, but the Promise offers us strength and assurance. It whispers to us in moments of uncertainty, urging us to press on with courage and trust.

In the quiet moments of reflection, we find solace in its unwavering presence, like a gentle hand on our shoulder, reminding us that we are never alone. As we journey forward, let us cherish the hope that blooms within us, ever resilient, ever bright, a testament to the enduring power of faith.

"Blessed are those whose strength is in You, whose hearts are set on pilgrimage."

—Psalm 84:5

He blesses the journeyer, not just the destination.

Along the winding paths of life, the journey itself is often filled with lessons, growth, and unexpected beauty. Each step taken in faith becomes a testament to resilience and courage. The traveler learns to cherish the small moments, finding joy in the whispers of nature, the kindness of strangers, and the quiet strength within. As hearts are set on pilgrimage, they are open to transformation and the discovery of new horizons. This sacred journey is a reminder that every road traveled with purpose and grace is a blessing, leading to destinations unknown yet deeply meaningful.

Prayer & Practice Prompt

Prayer

Lord, I thank You for the path behind and the presence ahead. I do not walk alone. Bless the burdens I carry, the people I meet, and the quiet spaces where You dwell. And when I grow tired, remind me—You are the road beneath my feet. Amen.

Practice

Take a final journal entry: What have you discovered in these pages about endurance, about God, and about yourself? Don't rush. Write it like a prayer or a letter. Let it be your personal benediction.

Pilgrim's Pause

Journaling Prompt:

What will you carry forward from this journey? What has changed in you—not outwardly, but inwardly?

As I reflect on my journey, I find that the most profound changes are those that occurred within. I've discovered a newfound resilience, a quiet strength that whispers encouragement in moments of doubt. This journey taught me the value of patience, the importance of embracing the present moment rather than rushing toward the future. I've learned to listen more intently, not just to others, but to the whispers of my own heart.

Empathy has deepened within me, allowing me to connect with others on a more compassionate level. I've come to understand that vulnerability is not a weakness but a bridge to deeper understanding and connection. My perspective has broadened, and I've learned to appreciate the small joys that sprinkle each day with light.

I carry forward a sense of gratitude, an appreciation for the lessons learned and the challenges overcome. The inner peace I've cultivated will guide me as I continue on life's path, reminding me that true transformation begins within.

Group Reflection:

What does it mean to bless one another as fellow pilgrims? How can we be reminders of grace in each other's journeys?

Blessing one another as fellow pilgrims means acknowledging and supporting each other's paths with kindness, empathy, and encouragement. It involves recognizing that each of us is on a unique journey, filled with its own challenges and triumphs, and choosing to walk alongside one another with open hearts and minds.

To be reminders of grace in each other's journeys, we can start by listening deeply and offering our presence without judgment. It's about celebrating each other's successes and providing comfort during challenging times. Simple acts of kindness, words of encouragement, and genuine compassion can uplift spirits and reinforce the bonds that connect us. By cultivating a community of mutual support and love, we create a nurturing environment where grace can flourish, allowing each of us to grow and thrive in our own way.

Afterword

Dear fellow pilgrim,

If you've walked this far, let me say this first: *you are not alone.*

These pages were never meant to impress. They were meant to walk beside. Through fog, fire, silence, or song—somewhere in your story, I pray these chapters found a familiar ache and whispered hope into it.

You didn't have to read them perfectly. You didn't need to agree with every word. You only needed to show up with a heart willing to keep going.

That, my friend, is **endurance**. And it is **holy**.

I don't know what weight you carry. I don't know what chapter of life holds you right now. But I believe this with all I am: "Your faithfulness matters." Not because of outcomes or accolades—but because you chose to continue when it would've been easier to stop.

That is sacred ground.

So, as you close these pages, may you walk lighter—not because the road is easier, but because you know you are seen, loved, and accompanied.

Let these words be your benediction, your lantern, your reminder:

"He who began a good work in you will carry it on to completion until the day of Christ Jesus."

—Philippians 1:6

May your path be watched over, your soul sustained, and your steps—no matter how faltering—be blessed.

Keep going.

With you on the road,

Charles E. Cravey

FOR FURTHER STUDIES OR BOOKS BY THE AUTHOR:

https://drcharlescravey.com

or Amazon.com/charles cravey books

FOR PROGRAMS OR INFO:

drrev@msn.com

www.ingramcontent.com/pod-product-compliance
Lightning Source LLC
LaVergne TN
LVHW041625070426
835507LV00008B/447